AFRICAN CHRISTMAS TRADITIONS

ISBN: 978-1-9162525-3-0

This activity book is a produced Infohubme, a social enterprise working to promote literary and cultural awareness among children, to build cultural tolerance among kids. To find out more about us, visit readgroofy.com.

Contact us: readingwithjoan@gmail.com

To you, Special one

Christmas is the best time of the year for me. I grew up with the smell of Christmas from the beginning of the last quarter of the year. I remember looking forward to my new Christmas dress and shoes, special jollof rice and other Christmas food exchanges with neighbours. Church services, nativity, and carols. The street parties and the fun games. Remembering thoughts produced a reflection of this African Christmas Traditions Activity book. I hope you dream of an African Christmas with me!

Joan Hephzibah

Content

- History of Christmas in Africa
- Christmas in Africa
- Christmas in Botswana
- Christmas in Ghana
- Christmas in Ethiopia
- Christmas in Mali
- Christmas in Kenya
- Christmas in Namibia
- Christmas in Nigeria
- Christmas in Zimbabwe
- Christmas in Chad
- Christmas in Congo
- Christmas in Egypt
- Christmas in Madagaskar
- Christmas in Mozambique
- Christmas in Tanzania
- Christmas in Cote d'ivoire
- Christmas in Zambia
- Christmas in Burkina Faso
- Christmas in Gambia
- Christmas in Sudan

Content

- Christmas in Burundi
- Christmas in Cameroon
- Christmas in Mauitius
- Christmas in Togo
- Christmas in Djibouti
- Christmas in Angola
- Christmas in Swaziland
- Christmas in Cape Verde
- Christmas in Morocco
- Christmas in Equatorial Guinea
- Christmas in Eritrea
- Christmas in Gabon
- Christmas in Lesotho
- Christmas in Liberia
- Christmas in Malawi
- Christmas in Rwanda
- Christmas in Senegal
- Christmas in Seychelles
- Christmas in Sierra Leone
- Countires without Christmas

History of Christmas in Africa

We all know the worldwide meaning of Christmas, on which people commemorate the birth of Christ in Bethlehem. Although historians are debating about the actual date of his birth, the overall accepted date is December 25th.

African history has an additional layer to the worldwide known account of Christmas. The earliest signs of Christian belief were found in Egypt in the 1st century AD. In many African countries, it symbolizes the birth of African God Ra (Osiris). So, when African people decorate trees during this period, they are sending regards to ancient times when Ra's birthday was celebrated. It is also considered the celebration of the winter solstice in some countries.

Since every African country has a distinct way of celebrating Christmas, let us take a closer look at some of these traditions.

South Africa is in the southern hemisphere, so the country celebrates Christmas during the hot summertime of the year. Combined with the fact that it is a public holiday, you will see a lot of people hanging out outside.

Many families go camping in massive tents, while those staying in cities organize outdoor events like traditional barbecue (braai). Families can opt for making braai on the grill or cook more traditional South African dishes.

Popular traditional dishes include turkey, duck, mince pie, roast beef, and pudding-like Plum pudding imported from the UK, and the locally invented Malva pudding.

The streets in the Cape Town and central districts are decorated with lights and inflatables. Also, most restaurants and shops will be closed since it is a national holiday, so most people do grocery shopping well in advance.

South Africa

- South Africa is in the _________________________.

- You will see a lot of people _______________ out outside.

- While those staying in cities organize outdoor events like traditional _______________.

- Popular traditional dishes include turkey, duck, mince pie, roast beef, and pudding-like _______ pudding imported from the _______.

- The streets in the _______________ and _________________ are decorated with lights and inflatables.

Name: ____

Date: ____

Word search puzzle.

Use 'Christmas in South Africa' information to search the words.

B	M	O	P	N	Q	T	P	S	G
A	D	U	P	U	D	D	I	N	G
R	A	S	L	I	T	O	R	L	T
B	O	G	R	I	L	L	K	L	U
E	C	A	P	E	T	O	W	N	R
C	B	T	V	A	U	X	A	P	K
U	R	V	D	U	C	K	K	L	E
E	A	O	C	A	P	E	T	U	Y
O	A	Y	B	N	Q	L	W	M	B
H	I	Z	C	A	M	P	I	N	G

DUCK, GRILL, PLUM, BRAAI, PUDDING, CAMPING, TURKEY, HOLIDAY, BARBECUE, CAPETOWN

Dear Santa!

My name is ___________________________.
I am _______________ years old.
This year I have been _______________ with family and friends.
For Christmas I would like

____

____

____

____

____

____

With love from _______________

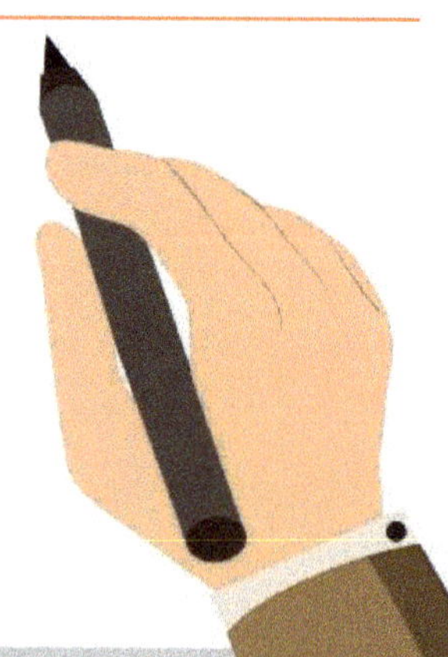

Botswana is in the Southern Hemisphere, so Christmas comes during the summer when it is very hot.

During the spring, families who own cows and goats take their livestock to live far away from their fields in a place called cattlepost. Some cows and goats always live at the cattleposts, but others are moved to the cattlepost in the spring and back to the village area in the fall.

About one third of people live in the cities of Gaborone, Francistown, Jwaneng and Lobatse. About a week before Christmas, most people from these cities travel back to their home villages. And then, people from the villages travel out to their cattleposts for several days after Christmas.

The churches in the villages have special services on Christmas Eve. On Christmas Eve, the church is usually more full than on any other day of the year. Sometimes three different choirs will sing during the Christmas Eve Service: the regular choir, the youth choir and a children's choir.

On Christmas Day, many people walk or drive out to their cattlepost. Each family's cattlepost is about six kilometres from the next family's cattlepost. The families go to visit other cattleposts and sing Christmas songs - acapella in beautiful four part harmony. The people of Botswana often

dance as they sing. Some choirs have new choir uniforms made before Christmas. Then the choir walks or drives from one cattlepost to another that are associated with their village singing for the different families.

Most families kill a goat or a cow at Christmas time and they enjoy eating a lot of meat during the Christmas holidays.

Some people will have a Christmas Tree, although this is a relatively new custom. Giving gifts is also popular but for most people gifts are home made. Often only rich people can afford to buy gifts for each other.

Magwinya (Fat Cakes) recipe

Ingredients

2 cups all-purpose flour

4 Tbsp white sugar

2 tsp instant yeast

1/2 tsp salt

1 Tbsp vegetable oil (plus more for frying)

2 cups warm water

Preparation

- In a large bowl, combine flour, sugar, yeast, and salt. Mix well.
- Add the water and 1 tablespoon vegetable oil and mix into a soft dough.
- Cover with a towel and allow to rise for one hour, at which point the dough should have doubled in size.
- Mix again and rest for an additional 10 minutes.
- Meanwhile, heat vegetable oil in a large pot over a medium flame for deep frying. Test with a drop of batter: when it sizzles, you're ready to fry.
- With a tablespoon, drop dollops of dough into the oil, using a second spoon to help push the dough down if necessary. Start with one magwinya at a time to practice your technique, turning frequently until golden brown.
- Drain over paper towels and serve as desired.

Christmas in Ghana

People in Ghana celebrate Christmas from the 20th of December to the first week in January with lots of different activities. Many people travel to visit their relatives and friends in other parts of the country. Over 66 languages are spoken in Ghana and all these language groups have their own traditions and customs!

December is also the start of the cocoa harvest (the bean that makes chocolate) in Ghana. Ghana is the worlds second biggest cocoa producer.

Christmas Eve night is the time when the celebrations really start with Church services that have drumming and dancing. Children often put on a Nativity Play or other drama. Then choirs come out to sing and people come out in front of the priests to dance. Songs are mostly sung in the languages that the people understand best. This makes them feel that God speaks their language. Sometimes these services and dancing go on all night long! Other people celebrate Christmas Eve with fireworks and parties.

On Christmas Day the Churches are very full. People come out dressed in their colorful traditional clothes. After the Church service on Christmas morning, people quickly go back to their houses to start giving and receiving gifts.

Traditional food includes stew or okra soup, porridge and meats, rice and a yam paste called 'fufu'.

Some Ghanaians also go to Church on the 31st December to thank God for sending Jesus and to pray for a good and safe New Year. People may also use that time to remember those who died during the previous year and pray that the difficulties that they may have encountered over the year don't carry on into the New Year.

Cassava And Plantain Fufu

This is a recipe for classic Ghanaian fufu based on cassava and plantain. After blending in a food processor, the mixture is cooked and steamed and can be served with literally any African soup, stew or sauce.

PLANTAIN

High in fiber and starch and low in fat, plantains are an unsweet banana variety which needs to be cooked before eating.

CASSAVA

This root, also called manioc or yuca, is one of the largest carbohydrates sources in the tropics, after rice and maize.

First, peel the plantain and cut it into cubes. Peel and scrape the cassava, de-string it and also cut into cubes.

Next, place the cassava and plantain into the blender. Add water: for now, use 350 ml if you want fufu to be firmer, or 450 ml if you prefer it softer.

Turn the blender on and process the ingredients into a smooth paste.

Next, heat the paste in a saucepan over medium heat. Stir constantly with a wooden spatula for 8 to 10 minutes to remove any lumps.

Now, add the remaining 50 ml of water to the mixture. Reduce the heat to the lowest setting, cover with a lid and steam for another 8 to 10 minutes.

After that, increase the heat to medium setting and stir. The fufu might look too soft, but it will become firmer as it cools down.

Transfer the fufu into a bowl and sprinkle one teaspoon of water on the surface to prevent forming a film. Let it cool completely.

Shape fufu into a ball and serve with soup or stew of your choice.

SERVING

After cooling, fufu is usually formed into a ball and served with soup, stew or sauce.

 **Use 'Christmas in Ghana' information to fill in the blanks.**

⭐ People in Ghana celebrate Christmas from the __________ of December to the first week in January with lots of different activities.

⭐ Ghana is the worlds second biggest ____________ producer.

⭐ Then choirs come out to sing and people come out in front of the ___________ to dance.

⭐ Songs are mostly sung in the languages that the ____________ understand best.

⭐ Other people celebrate Christmas Eve with _______________ and parties.

⭐ Traditional food includes stew or okra soup, porridge and meats, rice and a yam paste called _________.

⭐ Some Ghanaians also go to Church on the ____________st December

⭐ Thank God for sending _______________ and to pray for a good and safe New Year.

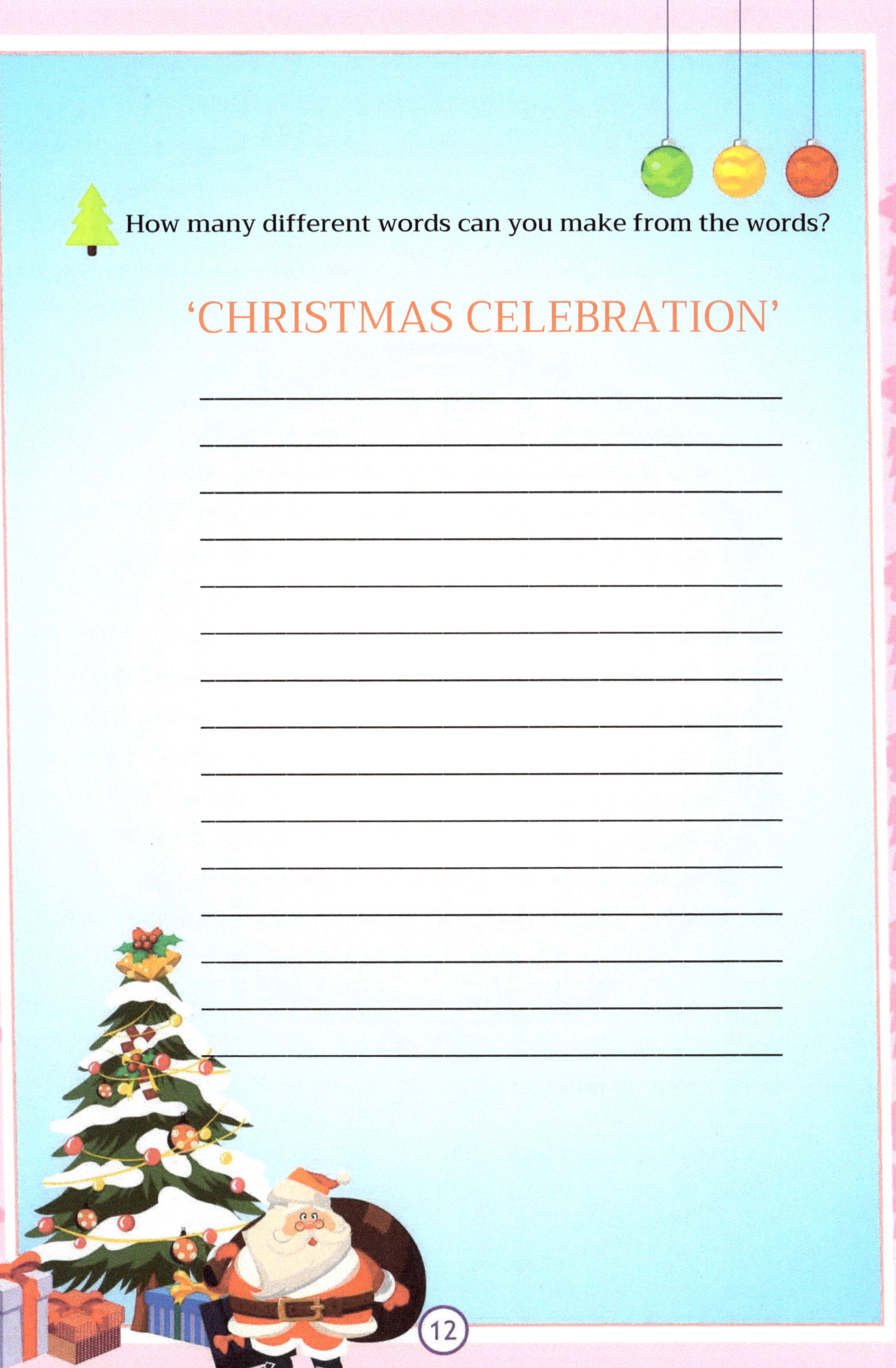

How many different words can you make from the words?

'CHRISTMAS CELEBRATION'

____
____
____
____
____
____
____
____
____
____
____
____
____

Christmas in Ethiopia

The Christmas celebration in the Ethiopian Orthodox Church is called Ganna or Genna. Most people go to Church on Christmas day.

Many people take part in a special Advent fast during the 43 days before Christmas. It starts on 25th November and is known as the 'Fast of the Prophets' (Tsome Nebiyat). During this time, traditionally only one vegan meal is eaten each day. It's a vegan meal because during the fast, foods including meat, dairy, eggs and wine aren't eaten.

For Ganna, people get dressed in white. Most people wear a traditional garment called a Netela. It's a thin white cotton piece of cloth with brightly coloured stripes across the ends. It's worn like a shawl or toga. If you live in a big town or city you might wear 'western' clothes. People go to church mass on Christmas Eve (called the gahad of Christmas) at 6.00pm and the service finishes about 3.00am on Christmas Day.

The choir sings from the outer circle. Everyone who goes to church for the Ganna celebrations is given a candle. The people walk around the church three times in a solemn procession, holding the candles. They then go to the second circle to stand during the service. The men and boys are separated from the women and girls. The centre circle is the most important and holy place in the church and is where the priest serves the Holy Communion or Mass.

Around the time of Ganna, the men and boys play a game that is also called ganna. It's played with a curved stick and a round wooden ball, a bit like hockey.

Traditional Christmas foods in Ethiopia include 'wat' which is a thick and spicy stew that contains meat, vegetables and sometimes eggs (sounds yummy!). Wat is eaten on a plate of 'injera' - a flat bread. Pieces of the injera are used as an edible spoon to scoop up the wat.

Twelve days after Ganna, on 19th January, Ethiopians start the three-day celebration of Timkat. It celebrates the baptism of Jesus. Children walk to church services in a procession. They wear the crowns and robes of the church youth groups that they belong to. Adults wear the Netela. The priests wear red and white robes and carry embroidered fringed umbrellas.

Musical instruments are played during the Timkat procession. The sistrum is a percussion instrument with tinkling metal disks a bit like a vertical tambourine. A makamiya, a long T-shaped prayer stick is used to keep the rhythm and is also used by the priests and a stick to lean on during the long Timkat church service!

People give and receive present during Ganna and Timkat. Sometimes children might be given a small gift of some clothes from their family members. It's more of time for going to church, eating lots and playing games!

Santa Claus is a fairly recent visitor to Ethiopia, only being known about through 'western' Christmas traditions. In the Amharic language, Father Christmas or Santa Claus is called 'Yágena Abāt' which means 'Christmas Father'.

How to Make a Paper Plate Christmas Tree Craft

You will need:

paper plate, green acrylic paint, paint brush, scissors, hole punch, ribbon or yarn, tape, stapler, brown cardstock paper or brown foam sheet, star foam sticker, sequins, small poms or embellishments, glue.

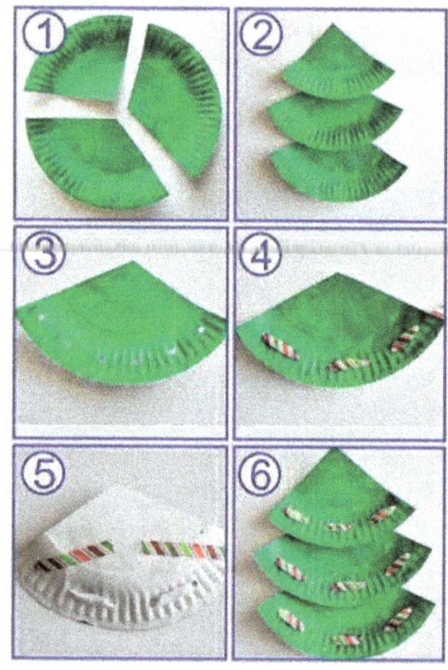

Instructions:

1. Start by painting your paper plate green. Let it dry completely.

2. When your paper plate is dry, cut it into thirds, then cut one of the section a bit smaller. When you layer them together with the smallest one on top, you have a Christmas Tree shape.

3. Use your hole punch to punch six (6) holes across the bottom of each paper plate section.

4. Cut a 12-inch section of ribbon for each paper plate section and lace them through the holes. Start by bringing the ribbon up from the back of the paper plate into the first hole and then continue through the holes, finishing with the excess ribbon hanging off the back of the paper plate.

5. Tape the excess pieces of ribbon to the back of the paper plate to hold them in place.

6. When you are finished lacing all your pieces, use a stapler to staple them together into your Christmas tree.

7. Finish your paper plate Christmas tree craft by stapling (or gluing) on a brown tree stump cut out from your brown paper and adding a foam star sticker at the top.

8. Glue on any sequin or embellishments that you would like to decorate your paper plate Christmas Tree craft. Such a beautiful piece of artwork to display for the holiday!

1. The Christmas celebration in the Ethiopian Orthodox Church is

   called _________________.

2. Many people take part in a special Advent fast during the

   ______ days before Christmas.

3. During this time, traditionally only one ___________ meal is

   eaten each day.

4. On Ganna, people get dressed in white. Most people wear a

   traditional garment called a ___________.

5. The Ethiopian capital city is _________________.

6. The people walk around the church three times in a

   ____________ procession, holding the candles.

7. Traditional Christmas foods in Ethiopia include _______ which

   is a thick and spicy stew that contains meat, vegetables and

   sometimes eggs.

8. Musical instruments are played during the _______________

   procession.

9. A _______________, a long T-shaped prayer stick is used to

   keep the rhythm and is also used by the priests

Christmas in Mali

Mali is a mainly Muslim country, but Christmas is also an official public holiday. In Mali, most Christmas celebrations take place in Churches, where people remember the real meaning of Christmas, that Jesus came into the world as a baby.

The festivities begin on Christmas Eve with an all night service which includes worship, preaching and items performed by different groups including children and young people. The children memorize Bible verses to recite on Christmas day at Church, as do the women. At the Christmas Eve service, each language group gets up and sings a song in their language.

There is often a baptismal service on the day after Christmas (Boxing Day), although this is sometimes held in the week before Christmas. Baptismal Services are special services where Christians make a public statement that they follow Jesus. This is normally done by being totally immersed (dunked) in water.

Some people can spend over 30 hours in Church over the Christmas period!

After Christmas the women's group of the Church often goes around to different courtyards (of houses) to greet people, sing and dance. The Church choir also does the same. If they come to your yard it is customary to give a small gift of money to the group. This is after Christmas Carol Singing!

Not many people give and receive presents at Christmas in Mali. It is only normally done by rich families.

Meni-meniyong

(Malinese Sesame-Honey Sweet)

Meni-meniyong is a wonderful Malinese sesame-honey sweet. It's easy to make and is great for kids and adults alike.

INGREDIENTS: Sesame seeds 1 cup, Honey 1 cup, Butter, unsalted 4 tablespoons

METHOD

1. Preheat oven to 450°F. Spread the sesame seeds on a baking sheet and toast in the oven for about 10 to 12 minutes. Remove and cool.

2. Heat the honey and butter in a small saucepan over medium-low heat, stirring until it bubbles and darkens somewhat, about 3 to 5 minutes.

3. Stir the toasted sesame seeds into honey mixture. Spread the mass onto a buttered baking sheet to a thickness of about 1/4 inch. Cool until it is just warm and break or cut into finger-sized pieces. Cool completely and serve.

MENI-MENIYONG VARIATIONS

For a tasty coating that will keep fingers less sticky, roll the candy in more toasted sesame seeds to coat after cutting it into pieces.

Unscramble letters

Make the correct word from the unscramble letter given below.

mhristcas ___________________

eelcbrotians ___________________

uejus ___________________

libbe ___________________

iaptbsm ___________________

hhurcc ___________________

oarcl ___________________

lami ___________________

Christmas in Kenya

In Kenya, Christmas is a time when families try and be with one another. Many people travel from cities, back to the villages where the main part of their family might live. (Although there are more whole big families now living in cities so they don't have to travel!) This is often the only time large families will see each other all year, so it is very important.

People try to be home for Christmas Eve, so they can help with the Christmas preparations. Houses and churches are often decorated with colorful balloons, ribbons, paper decorations, flowers and green leaves. For a Christmas Tree, some people will have a Cyprus tree.

In cities and large towns, stores can have fake snow outside them! And there might be a Santa in the stores as well.

In Kenya, Santa doesn't arrive with his Reindeer but might well come by Land-rover, Camel or even a bike!

Many people, especially Christians, will go to a Midnight Church Service to celebrate Christmas. The service will have Christmas hymns, carols & songs; and often nativity plays (showing the Christmas Story), poems & dances.

After the service, people go home and party really starts - you might well not sleep that night! In cities, going carol singing is also becoming more popular.

Some people will also go to Church on Christmas morning (if you haven't fallen asleep from partying all night!)

Popular Christmas foods include a barbecue which can be a goat, sheep, beef or chicken. This is eaten with rice and chapati flat bread. The big Christmas meal is called 'nyama choma'. People often make their own beer to drink and different tribes also have special dishes they make. If you live in a city you might have a western Christmas Cake, but these aren't very common in rural areas.

Only small gifts are normally exchanged and sometimes food and gifts are provided by missionary organisations.

The day after Christmas, Boxing Day, is also a public holiday in Kenya. It's another day of celebrating, seeing more friends and family (or sleeping!)

In Swahili/Kiswahili (a language spoken in Kenya) Happy/Merry Christmas is 'Heri ya Krismasi' and the response is 'Wewe pia' (you also). In the Maasai language (also called Maa or Kimaasai) it's 'nchipai e Kirismas'.

Christmas Cryptogram

 Use 'Christmas in Kenya' information to solve Christmas cryptogram.

Directions:

This is a cryptogram made easy for children. Boxes from A to Z are given with numbers.

The bottom part contains given in secret words. Take the letters from the above number and make the sentence words.

Here are the words to use in the empty space.

A	B	C	D	E	F	G	H	I	J	K	L	M	N	O	P	Q	R	S	T	U	V	W	X	Y	Z
9	5	17	23	8	6	20	4	2	26	1	10	18	3	25	11	21	24	19	15	13	16	12	7	22	14

d _ _ _ t _ _ _ _
23 8 17 25 24 9 15 2 25 3

_ _ b b _ _ _
24 2 5 5 25 3 19

_ _ _ o _ s _ _
5 9 10 10 25 25 3 19

_ r _ _ n
20 24 8 8 3

_ _ l _ _ _ _ l _
17 25 10 25 13 24 6 13 10

_ _ _ p _ s
17 22 11 24 13 19

p _ _ _ r
11 9 11 8 24

_ e _ _ s
10 8 9 16 8 19

_ l _ _ r
6 10 25 12 8 24

t _ _ e
15 24 8 8

colourful, balloons, ribbons, paper, decoration, flower, green, leaves, Cyprus tree

Santa and Kids Maze

 Santa wants to give gifts to the children, but he can't find a way. Will you find a way for Santa?

Christmas in Namibia

🟡 Namibia is in the Southern Hemisphere, so Christmas takes place during one of the hottest parts of the year. However, many Christmas traditions in Namibia come from Germany as it was a German colony between 1884 and 1915.

🟡 Christmas celebration start with Advent an advent crown is used in many churches and some homes (although as it's so hot often electric candles are used as wax ones can melt in the heat).

🟡 On St Nicholas' Day, 6th December, some children will hope for a visit from St Nicholas and there might be a St Nicholas party at schools. This is often the time that Christmas lights are switched on in the big towns and cities. As well as 'traditional' Christmas light decorations like snowmen and candles, you might also see Namibian animals like elephants!

🟡 Having a Christmas Tree is also popular. Some German speaking Namibians like to import pine trees from South Africa. But often a branch of a thorn tree is used instead. The tree is normally put up and decorated on Christmas Eve.

🟡 The main Christmas meal is also eaten on Christmas Eve. German style Christmas cookies, often made from gingerbread or marzipan, are popular to have with the

Following the Christmas Eve meal, it's common for people to go to a Midnight Mass service.

People from the parts of northern Namibia where the Oshiwambo language believe that Christmas is all about sharing. Their Christmas meals are often braais (barbecues) which are shared among family, friends and the local community.

People often travel back to their home villages from the cities to spend Christmas with their families. Having weddings at this time is also now becoming popular. Other people head to the coast of Namibia where it's a bit cooler - and you might even build a 'sandman' rather than a 'snowman'!

In Namibia, three of the main languages spoken are English, German and Afrikaans. So you can say 'Merry Christmas', 'Frohe Weihnachten' and 'Geseënde Kersfees'. Happy/Merry Christmas in lots more languages.

 Colour the Christmas candle in the right color scheme.

 # Gingerbread Cookies

This is a good Christmas recipe of Namibia

Ingredients:

2/3 cup shortening

1/2 cup brown sugar, packed

1 tsp cinnamon

1/4 tsp ground cloves

2 tsp ground ginger

pinch salt

3/4 cup molasses

1 egg

3 cups flour

1/2 tsp baking powder

1 tsp baking soda

Directions:

1) Collect all of the ingredients above and bring them to your work area along with 2 bowls for mixing, a measuring cup, measuring spoons, a tablespoon, a wooden spoon, an electric mixer, a cookie sheet, oven mitts and a spatula. 2) Use an electric mixer on medium speed to cream together the first 6 ingredients. 3) Add the egg and mix. 4) Add molasses and mix again. 5) Combine flour, baking powder and baking soda in a separate bowl. 6) Add the flour mixture to the creamed mixture about 1/4 cup at a time and stir until well blended. 7) Cover with saran wrap and chill for 1 hour. 8) Preheat oven to 375 F. 9) Roll out dough 1/4 at a time to 1/8" thickness or slightly thicker on a lightly floured board. 10) Cut with a cookie cutter and transfer to a non-stick cookie sheet. 11) Repeat with remaining dough. Before baking, decorate with raisins as you like. 12) Place in oven for 8 - 10 minutes. 13) While the cookies are baking, tidy your work area. 14) Cool on a wire rack. 15) Decorate with icing, m&m's, chocolate chips or any other items you wish.

Letter to Santa

Dear Santa!

My name is _________________________.

I am _____________ years old.

This year I have been _______________ with family and friends.

For Christmas I would like

____

____

____

____

____

____

____

____

With love from _______________

Christmas in Uganda

★ The proper name for Christmas in Uganda is Sekukkulu. In the Ugandan cities, the churches became the centre of the celebrations with church bells and carols by candlelight.

★ The churches hold ceremonies and events during the day. Many people visit churches with their fanciest clothes that they bought by saving up money for months. There are dance and singing performances, competitions and football matches all over the city.

★ In the evening, large dinner parties are organized, especially for the poor who can't afford many meals in daily life. Christmas meals are usually slow-cooked one day in advance. Matooke is an essential ingredient in the meals as in indigenous fruit that is steamed and mashed.

★ Interestingly, children of Uganda don't believe in Santa Claus, which is why they never expect gifts. People who live in rural areas try their best with the available resources like food and electricity to be part of the Christmas celebration.

 # Solve the Christmas Puzzle

Here is a tiny puzzle. Can you match pieces below in the right order? write 1,2,3,4,5,6,7,8,9 in the little circles alongside.

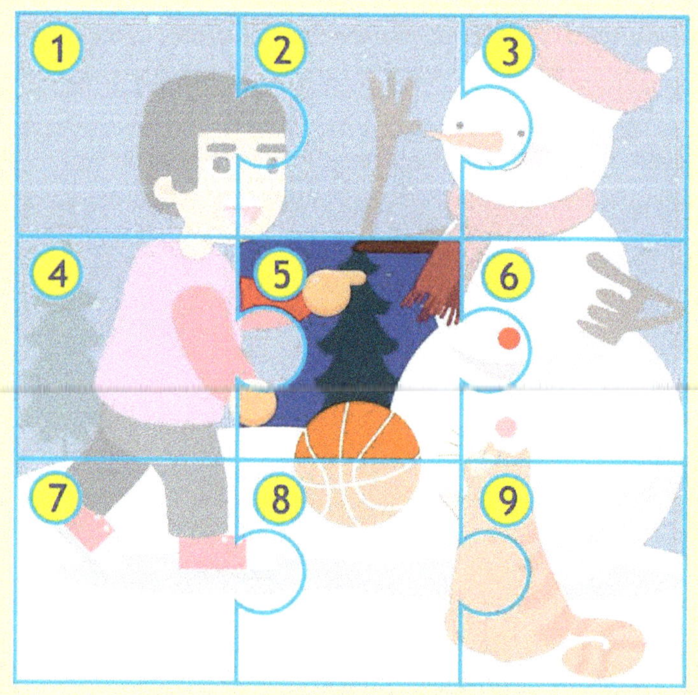

🎁 List objects in alphabetic order

Look at the objects in the picture, and list five of them
in alphabetical order.

Streamer
Christmas tree
Santa Caps
Bigul
Balloons

Christmas in Nigeria

Christmas is one of the most festive times in Nigeria, and it is time people spend with their families to show appreciation to their loved ones.

One of the most exciting advantages of living in Nigeria is that you will get to observe both Christian and Muslim holidays since those are the two primary religions in the country.

Most Christian households go to church service is held on Christmas morning to celebrate the birth of Christ. After visiting the church, the celebration starts with a traditional Christmas dinner party. Of course, there are several variations to celebrating an African Christmas, depending on if you are single, have a family, or the elderly.

Typically, smaller families can celebrate Christmas day with other families. They usually have grandparents from the countryside to be part of this special day.

In a larger family, one family member hosts the celebration, and kids, grandkids, parents, grandparents, friends and families, and people in the community are invited to come to have fun.

The most commonly prepared main dish consists of turkey, goat, sheep, or chicken, and side dishes range from fried rice to jollof rice, skewed beef (suya), and vegetable salads.

Also, depending on what tribe a family is from, they will make meals from their trip. You can see a list of the most popular Nigerian food during the festive season.

Community service is also a considerable part of an African Christmas in Nigeria. Church congregations play a crucial role by organizing events to visit the orphanages, adult family, and homeless homes, to visit the families and children.

The church members come with gifts, food, and drink, and the choirs will perform Christmas songs in many languages like Yoruba, Fulani, and Igbo.

Boxing Day is the day after Christmas when the wise men went to visit Jesus. In traditional churches in Nigeria, the church go on a short trip as a way to replicate the visit of the wise men. When they get to the location, usually a park with a lot of open space, they start the love feast.

The love feast is a ceremony where people come as they are to eat, drink, and be merry. A vital component of the love feast is a gift exchange. No matter how inexpensive a gift item is, everyone has to participate.

You exchange your wrapped gift with your church family and friends and establish new friendships during the process. Other activities during love feast include singing, dancing, Bible recitation.

 Make your own **CHRISTMAS** banner

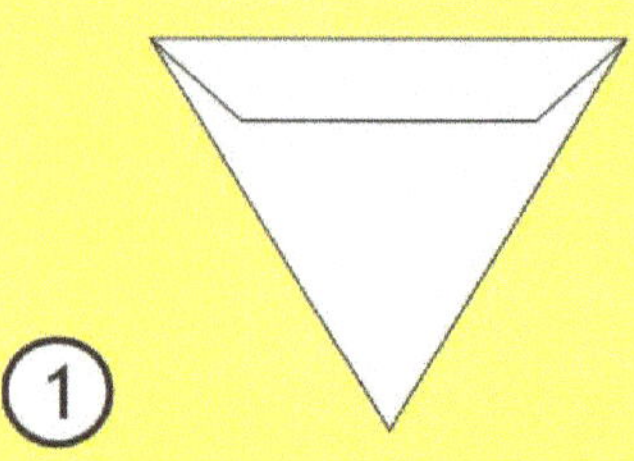

1 After the pieces have been colored, have a grown-up cut and fold the triangles. You will need a 5-foot piece of string, ribbon or yarn and some tape.

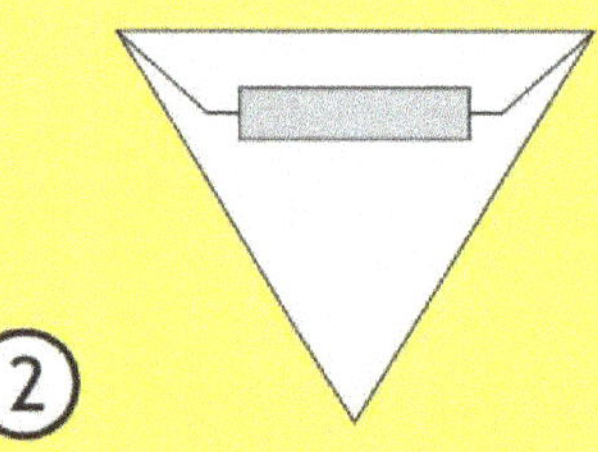

2 Tape each triangle to your piece of yarn securely. Make sure the piece doesn't slide around.

3 Have a grown-up help tape or pin your banner up in your room, across a big window, or on your Christmas tree! If the weather is good you can even hang it outside!

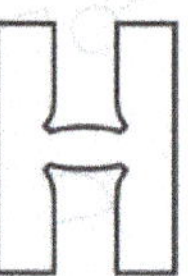

 Join dots and complete the santa's beard and colour it.

Christmas in Zimbabwe

For most people in Zimbabwe, Christmas day starts with a Church service. After the Church service, everyone has a party in their homes and people go from house to house, visiting all of their family and friends on the way home! Sometimes, this can take all of the rest of the day! At every house you have something to eat, exchange presents and enjoy the party.

A lot of people get their biggest stereo speakers out and put them outside the front of the house and play their favorite music very loudly! It is not only Christmas music that is played, but also the latest pop tunes and old African favorites.

Everyone wears their best clothes for Christmas, as for some families, the only new clothes they get every year are for Christmas. The parties are a good place to show off their new clothes.

Children in Zimbabwe believe that Santa Claus brings them there presents early on Christmas Day, ready to show their friends at Church and at the parties.

Only the main room in the house is often decorated in Zimbabwe. Some Zimbabweans have a traditional 'European' Christmas Tree, but they decorate the room with plants like Ivy. This is draped around the whole of the top of room.

Christmas Carols are sung during the Christmas Day morning service and in services leading up to Christmas. There

are also sometimes Carols by Candlelight Services in city parks.

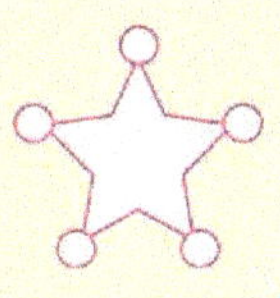

The Christmas Cards that are used in Zimbabwe sometimes have African pictures on them, such as wild animals, but most are imported so they have the traditional 'snow scenes' and pictures of the Christmas story on them.

The special food eaten at Christmas in Zimbabwe is Chicken with rice. Chicken is a very expensive food in Zimbabwe and is a special treat for Christmas. This is often eaten at the Christmas Day parties.

Santa might sometimes arrive at big stores in a Fire Engine. The streets in the big cities also can have colorful Christmas lights.

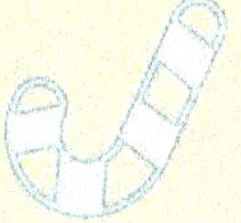

 # Create Snowglobes from Mason Jars

What You'll Need
Tree ornament
Glitter (2 tablespoons per globe)
Clear glue (2 ounces per globe)
Warm water (1 cup per globe)
Mason jar
Spoon
Glue gun

Step 1: Secure Your Ornament to The Lid

Using a glue gun, carefully glue the bottom of your tree ornament to the mason jar lid. Make sure to use enough glue to secure the ornament. Set aside to dry.

Step 2: Add Clear Glue to Your Jar

Add approximately 2 ounces of clear glue into your jar.

Step 3: Add Warm Water and Stir

Pour 1 cup of warm water into your jar and stir the mixture with a spoon.

Step 4: Add Glitter and Stir

Pour in 2 tablespoons of glitter (silver or white glitter works best). Then stir thoroughly with a spoon.

Step 5: Place the Lid

Take the lid with your ornament and place it face down into the mason jar. The lid should rest evenly on the

Step 6: Seal the Jar Tightly

Take the outer piece of the jar's lid and secure it tightly. Give it an extra twist to ensure the jar is tightly sealed. Add glue to the lid to prevent any leaking if needed.

Step 7: Shake and Enjoy!

Make sure your snow globe is completely sealed by shaking it carefully at first.

 Below are two pictures which are similar. But there are 7 differences, can you find them?

Christmas in Benin

- A country in West Africa

- Benin as a country is not as financially secure as other nations in Africa.

- So, some traditions that were adopted by other parts of Africa have not been used by the Beninese due to certain lack of resources as such....

- Masquerading is an ageless feature in lives of African People

- Though the languages throughout Africa differ it is referred to as Mmanwu throughout the continent.

- Benin is a primarily catholic country so much the Christmas day is spent either in a mass ceremony or in church.

- In Benin it is a custom to perform certain activities during the holiday season which singing and dancing to traditional Benin music featuring drums and chanting.

- It is a day off for the general population, and schools and most businesses are closed. Many people celebrate Christmas Day with a festive meal.

1. Snow man
2. Drum
3. Gingerbread
4. Bell
5. Ornaments
6. Holly
7. Candle

8. Stocking
9. Santa Cap
10. Present
11. Star
12. Christmas tree
13. Snow flakes
14. Candy

Trace this picture. and colour it.

Christmas in Chad

Although Chad is predominantly Muslim, they do celebrate Christmas. Compared to the previous countries on the list, Chad has the least westernized Christmas traditions. You will barely see any Christmas trees or fancy Christmas lights. Buying gifts is also quite rare since people cannot afford it.

There are so many different ways to celebrate the birth of Christ – every culture does it differently but the experience reminded me that it's the same God we are celebrating.

The morning of Christmas is spent at a traditional breakfast called millet. The supper is usually served with lamb or sheep. For Chadians, spending time with family is the most crucial aspect of Christmas, and they do that indoors, so you are less likely to encounter outdoor events.

The Christmas meal breaking off a small amount of boule (pounded ground millet cooked with water) with our right hand - to dip in a communal bowl of sauce.

let's make Popsicle stick reindeer

Required items:

Popsicle sticks, Colour paper or card stock, Pompoms, Googly eyes, Cotton balls, Glue, Scissors

Step 1: Glue your popsicle sticks together accordingly as shown.

Step 2: Trace along the stick frame and cut our one red triangle, one brown triangle, and a couple of reindeer antlers from paper or card stock.

Step 3: Glue the pieces you just cut out on the right place as shown.

Step 4: Add googly eyes and red pompoms as nose on the face. Glue down cotton balls to make the brim of the hat.

 Here is a design outline of some of the Christmas
elements, you fill it with right colour scheme

Children Road safety

Match the correct picture with right thigs.

1. Don't play on the road.

2. Do not eat or drink while walking on the road.

3. Use the bridge when crossing the road.

4. Do not cross the railing on the sidewalk.

5. Zebra crossing when crossing the road.

6. Use footpath while walking outside.

7. Look around as you cross the road.

Christmas in Congo

🎁 Christmas in the Democratic Republic of the Congo is more of a religious festival rather than being commercial. Most people won't have any presents.

🎁 Christmas Eve is very important with Churches having big musical evenings (many churches have at least 5 or 6 choirs) and a nativity play. These plays last a very long time. They start at the beginning of the evening with the creation and the Garden of Eden and end with the story of King Herod killing the baby boys.

🎁 People taking part in the play really like to show off their 'best' acting skills and tend to go over the top and 'ham it up'! King Herod and the soldiers are often figures of fun (like pantomime 'baddies') and Mary is often well advanced in labor before she arrives!

🎁 The birth of Jesus is timed to happen as close to midnight as possible and after that come the shepherds, the wise men and the slaughter of the innocents. This means the play normally finishes about 1am. However, in some places there will be further singing until dawn! The Christmas day service then starts at 9am with lots more singing.

🎁 On Christmas day, most families try to have a better meal than usual. If they can afford it, they will have some meat (normally chicken or pork). The rest of the day is spent quite quietly, maybe sleeping after a busy and late night on Christmas Eve!

People go back to work on the 26th (Boxing Day).

Santa does 'NOT FORGET'

This story is about a boy who lives with his father and mother. He's kind and obedient and shares all of his toys with his friends. However, he made a mistake: he always forgot to do odd jobs and other important jobs he was asked to do. Every time he is asked to do something and then asked, he has an answer, "I forgot." If he was sent to the tailor to remind him of an urgent change, he would forget to tell the tailor about it. If he were given money to pay for electricity, his mother would find the money and bills in his pocket that every night. The reason for not doing a specific job remains the same. You guessed it right – "I forgot."

Parents worry that this forgetful habit will affect the boy's adult life, making it difficult for him. They decide to do something about it to make him remember everything. Christmas is coming, and like the other children, the boy is busy preparing the bill for Santa Claus, asking for his favorite items. His mother said, "Santa might forget to bring those for you." But the boy is sure that Santa Claus will look like he will put them in his socks so he will leave the list.

On Christmas morning, he woke up early and hurriedly checked his socks, pretty sure Santa would deliver all he wanted. His mother knew what was going to happen and stayed away from him. The boy stood in front of his mother with a long list of all the jobs he had been asked to do during the past year. At the bottom of the list, bold text is written, "I FORGET".

The boy was heartbroken and dragged himself to visit his grandfather with the rest of the family. On his grandfather's Christmas tree, the boy finds everything he has always wanted! Even though he doesn't change immediately, his mom still reminds him when things are out of hand – "Santa doesn't forget!" He slowly understood why it was so important to remember one's duties and responsibilities in life.

✦ He's kind and obedient and shares all of his ___________ with his friends.

✦ Every time he is asked to do something and then asked, he has an answer, "___________."

✦ His mother would find the ___________ and ___________ in his pocket that every night.

✦ Parents worry that this ______________ habit will affect the boy's adult life, making it difficult for him.

✦ Christmas is coming, and like the other children, the boy is busy preparing the bill for______________

✦ Santa Claus will look like he will put them in his ____________ so he will leave the list.

✦ On _____________ morning, he woke up early and hurriedly checked his socks, pretty sure Santa would deliver all he wanted.

✦ The boy was ________________ and ______________ himself to visit his grandfather with the rest of the family.

✦ He slowly understood why it was so important to remember one's duties and __________________ in life.

Christmas in Egypt

⭐ In Egypt about 15% of people are Christians. They are the only part of the population who really celebrate Christmas as a religious festival. Most Egyptian Christians belong to the Coptic Orthodox Church and they have some very unique traditions for Christmas.

⭐ Christmas Day isn't celebrated on the 25th December but on 7th January (like in Ethiopia and by some Orthodox Christians in Russia and Serbia).

⭐ The Coptic month leading to Christmas is called Kiahk. People sing special praise songs on Saturday nights before the Sunday Service.

⭐ For the 43 days before Christmas (Advent), from 25th November to 6th January, Coptic Orthodox Christians have a special fast where they basically eat a vegan diet. They don't eat anything containing products that come from animals (including chicken, beef, milk and eggs). This is called 'The Holy Nativity Fast'. But if people are too weak or ill to fast properly they can be excused.

⭐ On Coptic Christmas Eve (6th January), Coptic Christians go to church for a special liturgy or Service. The services normally start about 10.30pm but some chapels will be open for people to pray from 10.00pm. Many people meet up with their friends and families in the churches from 9.00pm onwards. The services are normally finished shortly after midnight, but some go onto 4.00am!

⭐ When the Christmas service ends people go home to eat the big Christmas meal. All the foods contain meat, eggs and butter - all the yummy things they didn't during the Advent fast! One popular course is 'Fata' a lamb soup which contains bread, rice, garlic and boiled lamb meat.

⭐ On the Orthodox Christmas Day (7th) people come together in homes for parties and festivities. People often take 'kahk' (special sweet biscuits) with them to give as gifts.

⭐ Even though not many in Egypt are Christians, a lot of people in the country like to celebrate Christmas as a secular holiday. Christmas is becoming very commercial and most major supermarkets sell Christmas trees, Christmas food and decorations. Hotels, parks and streets are decorated for Christmas.

Christmas sweets are so yummy and delicious.
Name and draw your favorite Christmas sweets.

Christmas in Madagascar

Most people go to Church on Christmas Eve in Madagascar. The services start about 5.00pm and last until after midnight! Different groups in the Church, especially children, perform songs and plays celebrating the birth of Jesus. People also go to Church on Christmas Day as well. After the Christmas Eve or Christmas Day service, churches give out sweets or biscuits to the people in the Church.

Here are some Malagasy Christmas Carol!

Sambasamba Zanahary (Which means 'It's a big opportunity Lord that you send your only Son to save us from our sin')

Sambasamba, Zanahary

Tamin'ny nampidinanao

Ny Zanakao malalanao

Mba hisolo ny helokay

Tamin'ny nampidinanao

Ny Zanakao, malalanao, malalanao

Mba hisolo ny helokay

On Christmas Day people (even strangers) greet each by saying 'Arahaba tratry ny Noely' which means 'Merry Christmas'.

Malagasy families like to eat Christmas dinner together in large groups and dress up in the best (or new) clothes. The meal is normally Chicken or Pork with rice, followed by a special cake. Some rich people go to restaurants for Christmas dinner, but most people stay at home with their families. Here are some recipes from Madagascar.

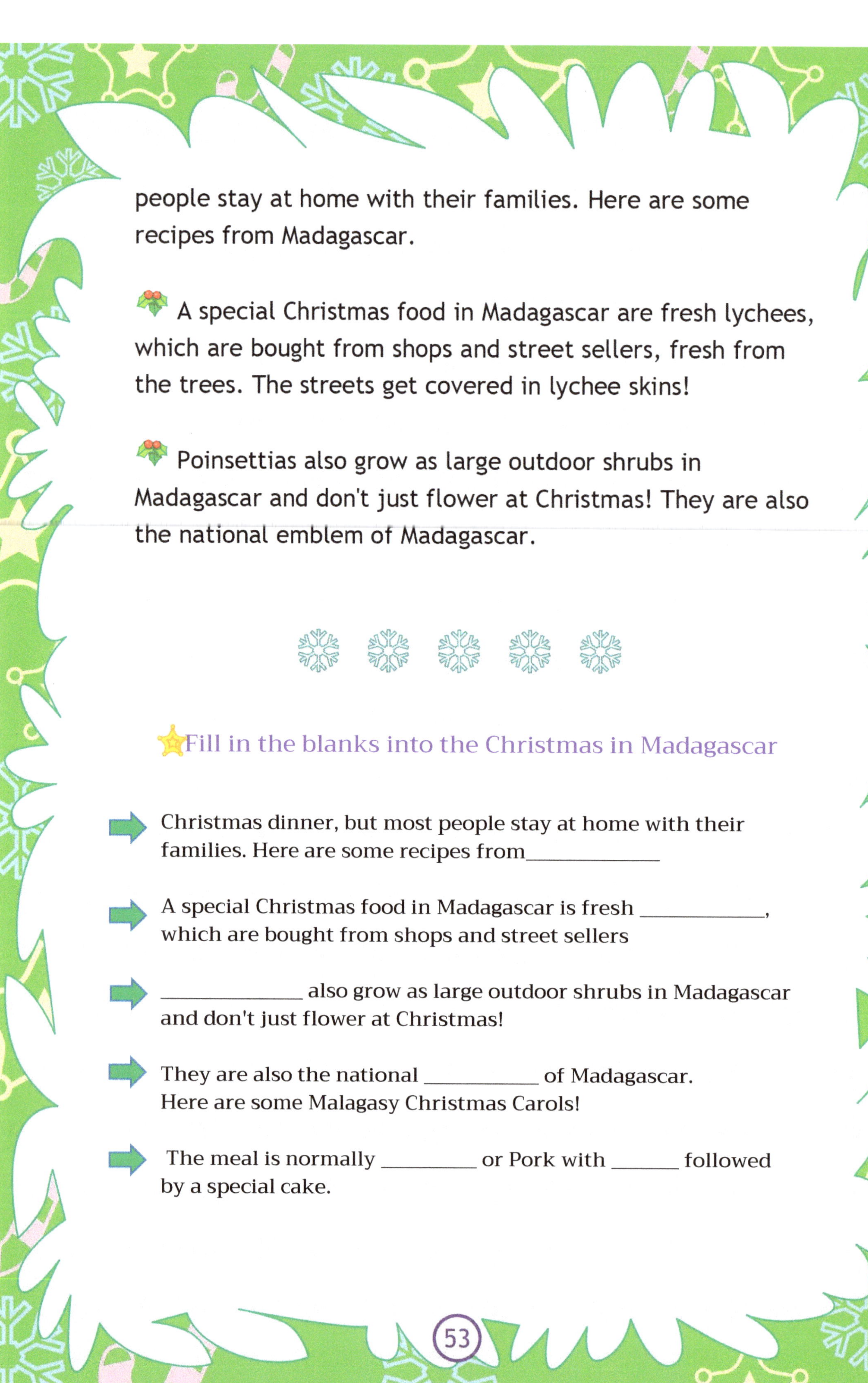

A special Christmas food in Madagascar are fresh lychees, which are bought from shops and street sellers, fresh from the trees. The streets get covered in lychee skins!

Poinsettias also grow as large outdoor shrubs in Madagascar and don't just flower at Christmas! They are also the national emblem of Madagascar.

❄ ❄ ❄ ❄ ❄

⭐Fill in the blanks into the Christmas in Madagascar

➡ Christmas dinner, but most people stay at home with their families. Here are some recipes from_____________

➡ A special Christmas food in Madagascar is fresh _____________, which are bought from shops and street sellers

➡ _____________ also grow as large outdoor shrubs in Madagascar and don't just flower at Christmas!

➡ They are also the national _____________ of Madagascar. Here are some Malagasy Christmas Carols!

➡ The meal is normally _________ or Pork with _______ followed by a special cake.

Colour and decorate the merry Christmas with collage art.

Christmas in Mozambique

For many Mozambicans, Christmas has not only a religious meaning, but also a social one. Through Christmas, family and friends come together to spend time together, eat together and celebrate.

People in Mozambique celebrate Christmas in high summer. The actual holiday in Mozambique is on December 25. In the Mozambican holiday calendar, it is also called "Family Day".

Most Christians spend the night from December 24 to 25 in church. There they celebrate the holy mass, the "Misa da noite do Natal", where they pray together, sing and celebrate the birth of Christ.

December 25 is celebrated in Mozambique with family and friends. Many Mozambicans spend the day either at the beach or at home in the garden or yard. Unlike December 24, on this special day the table is richly set. Each family brings homemade specialties that are festively arranged on a buffet.

On Christmas, many Mozambicans wear red dresses or robes.

Due to the proximity to Portugal and Brazil, the habit of gift-giving has become more and more established in Mozambique. During Advent, gifts are exchanged among friends, colleagues, and family members. In Germany, this tradition is known as "Wichteln" – or as they say in Mozambique: "Amigo oculto".

Setting up Christmas trees is also becoming increasingly popular. In Mozambique, however, mainly artificial trees are bought. Traditionally, the houses are not decorated with fairy lights as we know it, for example, in Germany. Rather, the stores in the city centre are illuminated or the houses of those who can afford it. The Advent calendar is also not widespread in Mozambique, not yet at least, since the western influence is spreading more and more in the African country.

The Christmas Dinner in Mozambique

Traditionally in Mozambique, as in Portugal, boiled cod is eaten on Christmas Eve with boiled potatoes, vegetables, and eggs. The cod is imported from Portugal for this purpose. For dessert, there is a simple homemade cake (pão de lò) and cashews roasted on charcoal.

 Stick a beautiful photo of your family in the frame below and wish your family a Merry Christmas below.

Make a Popsicle stick Santa

Supplies you need:

Popsicle sticks

Color paper or card stock

Pompoms

Googly eyes

Cotton balls

Glue

Step 1: Glue your popsicle sticks together accordingly as shown.

Step 2: Trace along the stick frame and cut out 2 white triangles and 1 small red triangle from paper or card stock.

Step 3: Glue those three triangles on the right place as shown.

Step 4: Add googly eyes and red pompom as a nose on the face with glue. Add white pompom on the hat with glue.

Step 5: Glue cotton balls on the bottom triangle as the beard.

Christmas in Tanzania

Nearly one-third of Tanzanians are Christian, so Christmas in Tanzania is a big deal – but it's not so much about the buy frenzy that occurs elsewhere. But it does share the global tradition of families getting together because many Tanzanian families are separated for much of the year, with parents and grandparents living back in villages and the young far away in towns and cities.

So, it's a special time for families, and with most vacation starting two weeks before Christmas, you'll see people on the road, heading back to villages to share Christmas with mum, dad and grandma.

Like many families the world over, Tanzanian families get together for Christmas. It's a time of catching up, feasting, quarrelling, playing and chilling out. But, in a culture where it's not easy to meet up throughout the year, it's a perfect opportunity for the family to get to know a new family member such a new wife, husband or child, and also reconnect with extended family like long lost cousins.

A few days before Christmas there's a frenzy as Christmas decoration are taken out of boxes, dusted down and put up. Many decorations are made from recycled materials, like recycled bottles.

Being a celebration, families will often buy a cow or goat in January just to feed it up in time for Christmas. It's traditional to kill the animal on Christmas Eve and prepare its supu (offal) and makorongo (legs) to eat that evening.

Many villages brew their own beer and whole tribes create their own brands. For instance, the Chagga tribe brews Mbege, brewed from bananas and sprouted millet, which has a wine-like quality. The beer comes out on Christmas Eve to accompany the meat, and we'd be lying if we said that everyone stays sober.

It's a custom to kit out children with new clothes at Christmas time – whether these have been bought at a market or hand-sewn from a pattern based on existing clothes or something different. Children expect new clothes at Christmas and it's an exciting time for them so parents always try their best not to disappoint! For some children, these are the only new clothes they receive all year.

Going to church on Christmas Day is very common and many people leave home early in the morning, dressed up in new clothes, to celebrate in the community. The church service can take up much of the morning with some services as long as two hours, but you'll be back in time for lunch.

Christmas means a whole lot of singing, too! Children sing traditional Christmas songs in Swahili and there are also carols sung in English, too. Everyone will sing Christmas songs during the church service and afterwards, too.

In Tanzania, some meals are venerated and preparing and eating them is a sign of a really good Christmas. Swahili Pilau – spicy rice'n'meat – and chapati are traditional fare. Don't forget to try making it for yourself – see our recipe below. It's a secret family recipe.

It's not just about food and drink. Christmas dinner in Tanzania is about a family getting together and sharing a meal, making happy

Planting is a great thing,

But 5 things are wrong in this picture.

Can you find them?

1. _______________________________

2. _______________________________

3. _______________________________

4. _______________________________

5. _______________________________

Christmas in Cote d'ivoire

🎩 The city of Abidjan has a festival of lights called Perle des Lumiéres.

🎩 The Ivoirian's usually celebrate by going to a midnight mass.

🎩 During a traditional mass there are lots of dancing, singing, and children show off little plays or skits they've been working on.

🎩 The men, women, and children wear traditional bright clothing for the service.

🎩 After the mass is over (6:00 A.M.), the people take about an hour to get ready and change clothes before they have a traditional meal to break their fast called a Reveillon.

🎩 Reveillon consists of traditional foods such as fufu and chilled avocado soup.

🎩 A yule log may be present for after the main meal.

Santa claus	Cake
Christmas tree	Bell
Reindeer	Cap
Cup	Song
Jingle	Cookie
Balloons	Sleigh
Carol	Ornaments
Gingerbread	Decorations

Write information about how you are going to celebrate Christmas.

Christmas in Zambia

🎄 Many churches in Zambia have nativity plays and a crib in the church.

🎄 One or two days before Christmas, Zambians like to go carol singing around the local streets for charity.

🎄 On Christmas day, children are encouraged to bring a present to church for children who are in hospital or might not get a present because they are less fortunate.

🎄 After church, on Christmas day, it is a custom that all the children go to one house and all the adults go to another house to have a party and to eat!

 # The Elves and the Shoemaker

'The Elves and the Shoemaker' is a classic Christmas fairy tale. This tale by the 'Brothers Grimm is about two elves that sneakily help a poor shoemaker.' This story is about a shoemaker who lives with his wife in a small house. He is very poor and doesn't have any money left for him. He only has some leather left to make one pair of shoes. One evening, he cut the leather for a pair of shoes that he thought he would make in the morning, and prayed to God for a good day and goes to sleep. The next morning, the shoemaker finds a beautiful pair of shoes on the table in his shop and sells it for a hefty price.

For many days, this continues and the shoemaker turns rich by selling the shoes made by the elves. The shoemaker and his wife are pleased; they decide to find out who their helpers are and express their gratitude towards them. They make clothes for the elves in order to thank them for their service. The two little elves come at midnight and are happy to see the clothes. They wear it and go only to never return again.

The shoemaker lives a happy and prosperous life thereafter, and little elves are pleased, too. This is a remarkable story to teach your children about the importance of hard work. Hard work always reaps its rewards. It is because the shoemaker worked hard that the elves came to help him. In return, he also gave the elves wonderful new clothes made with love.

Q. Who writes 'The Elves and the Shoemaker' story?

____

____

Q. Shoemaker what used to make by cutting leather?

____

____

Q. What does shoemaker see on the table when he wakes

up in the morning?

____

____

- For many days, this continues, and the shoemaker turns rich by _______________ the shoes made by the elves.

- They make clothes for the elves in order to thank them for their _____________.

- In return, he also gave the elves wonderful new _____________ made with love.

Christmas in Burkina Faso

🎄 Christmas in Burkina Faso is celebrated on December 25th. Christmas in this country is typically celebrated both among families and in churches.

🎄 Christmas is not about decorations or gifts for children, but is about supplying good food for family and neighbours.

🎄 In Burkinabe villages, children mix clay, straw and water to build masterpieces outside of their compounds, illustrating the biblical theme of the crib.

🎄 Mary, Joseph and the baby Jesus are clay figures made inside of the clay-crib.

🎄 Less than half the people in Burkina Faso are Christian. Most of the others are Muslim. In the same way, the Christians prepare a big feast for Christmas and Easter and the Muslims come to share the feasts with them. Togetherness is the focus of holiday celebrations in the country.

🎄 Families in Burkina Faso may celebrate the holiday with a special meal of chicken or mutton.

🎄 Families usually skip having rice with their meals on Christmas because they have rice every day throughout the rest of the year. Instead, they substitute macaroni for rice.

🎄 After church on Christmas, many people in Burkina Faso stay up late dancing and partying for the holidays, and sometimes these festivities even include fireworks.

Complete the crossword according to the Christmas related things given here.

SLEIGH, HOLLY, CANDLE, CANDY, REINDEER, BELLS, CAROLS, GINGERBREAD, WINTER, PRESENT, XMAS, SANTA

Do you know what to do in an emergency? Talk about it with your family. Fill in this page and put it near your phone.

My Phone Number _______________________

My Address _______________________

____

Father's Phone Number _______________________

Mother's Phone Number _______________________

Brother's Phone Number _______________________

Sister's Phone Number _______________________

Police _______________________

Fire _______________________

Poison Control _______________________

Doctor _______________________

Dentist _______________________

Neighbors _______________________

My School Phone Number _______________________

Christmas in Gambia

About 9% of population is Christian in the Gambia, that is also the reason, Christmas is celebrated, not only amongst the Christians but also some Muslims. Christmassy spirit starts after 15th of December when hear the first carols on the street. Many choirs from different churches start going from one house to another, singing Christmas carols, bringing the Christmas spirit and blessing, while collecting voluntary contributions in return. Many times, especially at the beginning of this period, choirs from different churches gather and perform in the certain church, preparing their special repertoire, impressing the crowd. Carolling lasts till the Christmas eve or maybe a day or two less.

Another tradition is building of a "fannal" or so-called paper boat, which is built of long bamboo sticks and decorative paper, usually also beautified with some candles or electric lights. It can be up to 10 m long and it is used for parade, which is accompanied by some drummers, singers and dancers going around, spreading good energy and holiday mood.

Churches and also people usually share gifts, especially amongst those in need. They are provide clothes or food, mostly oil, rice, sugar, onion and also soap for clothes washing. Sometimes, church decide to help a hospital or orphanage. It is all about the sharing and helping one another. In the times before the Christmas, there are also many trade fairs organised, where people sell their products, there are face painting and other fun activities for the kids, all accompanied with some festive music.

On the Christmas eve, everybody goes to the church since there is usually long and beautiful program included in the Christmas eve mass. There are carolling of the different church choirs. Depending on the church, the program would end at 10 pm and in some, even after the midnight. After the mass, celebration begins. Even though is mostly at homes, with family members or smaller group of relatives, this doesn't mean the party is not going. There is a lot of dancing, singing and especially food. The one hosting has to prepare plenty of dishes to satisfy all the guests and members on this special day. In case there is too much of liquid Christmas spirit during the celebration, there is cow foot pepper soup waiting for anyone to cool the head and continue with the celebration, which can end up at 3 or even 5 o'clock in the morning!

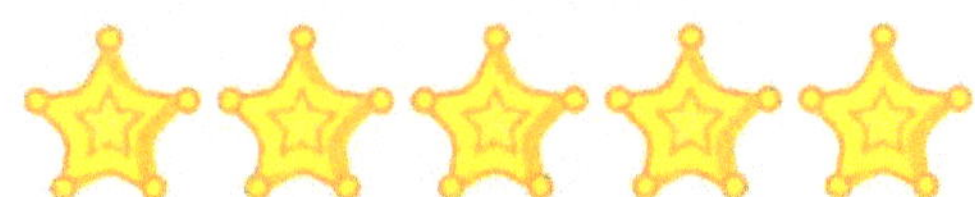

TASK GAME

Here is a task game. It is a ludo type game. dice used to play.

| START | ● | dance | ● | singing | ● |

Popsicle stick Christmas tree

Supplies you need:

Popsicle sticks,

Colour paper or card stock,

Pompoms,

Googly eyes,

Cotton balls,

Glue,

Scissors

Direction:

Step 1: Glue your popsicle sticks together accordingly, as shown.

Step 2: Trace and cut out one green triangle from paper or card stock and glue it on the right place.

Step 3: Cut out some green mosaics and a yellow star. Glue the green mosaics on the stick frame and glue the yellow star on the top of frame.

Step 4: Add some coloured pompoms as lights on the Christmas tree.

Christmas in Sudan

Sudan, the largest country in Africa, is an ethnically and religiously diverse society. About 70 percentage of its citizens are Muslim and some claim Arab roots. They live mostly in the north. About 25 percentage of Sudanese follow tribal religions and about five percentage are Christians.

Sudanese Christians still celebrate Christmas. Their celebrations might seem unfamiliar to many Americans, however. They never adopted the western European custom of decorating a Christmas tree. The American Santa Claus and other Christmas gift bringers are unknown to them.

In much of war-torn southern Sudan, Christians simply hope to celebrate Christmas by attending church and sharing a good meal with their family. Christmas church services in Sudan include readings from the Bible as well as many hymns written in tribal languages such as Nuer, Dinka, Shilluk, Naban, Zande, Baria, and Tira. Hymn singing is often accompanied by drumming and sometimes by dancing.

One foreign aid worker described a moving Christmas Eve service attended by many refugees in which the sermon pointed out that Jesus came into the world as a refugee, his parents forced to leave their homes to fulfil the demands of a hostile government. People who can afford it wear new clothes on Christmas Day. Dance parties, featuring traditional tribal dress and dancing, also take place at Christmas time.

Animal Research
Animal name
PICTURE
FACTS
OTHER INFO
HABIBAT
76

Make A DiY Mason Jar Terrarium

You'll need:

Mason jar (we used a recycled pickle jar)

Small plant (like a succulent)

Potting soil (choose the most appropriate soil for your plant)

Pebbles, rocks, sand and moss (you can find these at a garden centre)

Step 1

Start adding your layers and work up from large to small. We started with bigger rocks and a layer of moss for drainage and colour.

Step 2

Work up to your soil layer. All the pebble and moss layers create, drainage since your glass jar doesn't have any holes at the bottom—this will help prevent over-watering the plant. Add 1-2 inches of soil. (If you add too much, it will trap moisture and all the work you did with your layers won't be effective).

Step 3

Dig a little hole in the soil, loosen the roots and add your plant. Finish with a final layer of moss. Water the moss and not the plant. Succulents prefer to keep their leaves dry (they won't be offended if you neglect them a little).

Step 4

For an adorable final touch, print out pics of your kids and tape a toothpick on the back. Don't forget the little gnome hat-cut out of a piece of red felt and glue on. Tip: Remove your little gnomes when you water the plant.

Christmas in Burundi

On Christmas day, everyone would go to church. In Burundi choirs sing Christmas carols in church services, and some Christmas services can be very long. Christmas day is spent with family and friends enjoying good things to eat and drink.

In Burundi, people celebrate Christmas all day long.

In Burundi choirs sing Christmas carols in church services, and some Christmas services can be very long. Christmas day is spent with family and friends enjoying good things to eat and drink.

Here's Snowman outline. Can you colour it?

Here's what kids should and shouldn't do. There are pictures, but no text message. Will you write it?

Christmas in Cameroon

Christmas is one of the most important days of the year in Cameroon. There is a large Christian population in the country, around 70% of people in Cameroon are Christian, so it's a widely celebrated event throughout the nation. The tradition of celebrating Christmas in Cameroon is a product of French and British influence from the country's colonial past, and there are certain similarities between Western and Cameroonian Christmas festivities.

Due to the large population of Christians in Cameroon, celebrations in many communities are religious or spiritual in nature. The act of going to church is of major importance during Christmas in Cameroon, and many take part in several services over the festive period, from carol singing to a candlelit service on Christmas Eve. Children get a week of school holiday before Christmas, and lots of families seize the opportunity to reunite and celebrate by having a day out to places like the zoo or botanic gardens.

Much like Christmas in the west, decorating can be a cause of huge excitement during the festive period in Cameroon. Many families rush to decorate areas in their communities with anything they can, from lights in their homes to candles and a nativity scene in local churches. The centrepiece decoration of many homes, though, is a Christmas tree, and it comes with a Cameroonian twist. Although plastic evergreen-inspired Christmas trees are becoming more

popular in the country, the traditional Christmas tree in Cameroon is the local Cypress tree which can be found decorated with banana leaf and orange ornaments.

No Christmas is complete without a festive feast. This is especially true for many celebrating Christmas in Cameroon, where it's an opportunity for families to reunite and enjoy themselves over a delicious meal. As with their Christmas trees, the food served for Christmas dinner is uniquely Cameroonian.

The most common Christmas dinner you're likely to find in Cameroon won't include turkey, but chicken and the main bulk of the meal won't be roast potatoes, but rice. Other dishes that are common at Christmas are fufu (a dough made out of plantain, cassava or yams), Achu soup (yellow soup made from cocoyam) and ndolé (a nut and ndoleh stew). While some western influences can be found in festive desserts like plum puddings eaten in Anglophone regions and Bûche de Noël (yule logs) in Francophone regions, in many communities, especially in rural areas, such delicacies can't be afforded.

Can you help kids to reach the Christmas tree.

Christmas in Mauritius

Traditionally, Christmas gifts are offered to kids and young people and is placed under the warmly decorated Xmas Tree. Gifts are opened in the morning on Christmas day and most kids believe in Father Christmas. Christmas day is a public holiday marked by family gatherings at home or at the beach.

The flamboyant trees with their reddish orange flowers during the month of December herald the Christmas festivities in Mauritius. Christmas carols are played on all radio stations, whether in the city or in rural areas, the island has managed to preserve this atmosphere that is typical of the season, where the streets reveal storefronts and windows that compete in creativity through decoration,

Mauritians from all communities on the island, from all social strata, are taking advantage of this favourable month to spend the end of the year holidays with their families and also to shop until very late at night. Although Christmas is primarily a Christian celebration, it is considered as a national celebration in Mauritius since it brings families back together for a good and enjoyable meal.

In churches as well as in shopping malls you can enjoy the Christmas carols at the corner of the nativity scene, there are something for everyone!

only a few days before Christmas on the main streets, although in recent years the artificial tree has gained ground not only for its practicality but also for ecological reasons. While Christmas shopping is done for the youngest and oldest, the menu is prepared well before Christmas Eve. While Santa Claus is on his way to the tropics, others gather in churches to relive the birth of Christ during vigils in an atmosphere as prayerful as it is joyful in the light of candles. Whether during the day or in the evening, the Mauritian Christmas meal is a joyful blend of European, Asian and Creole cultures that reflects the people. While the older ones feast, the younger ones will go to bed quietly but with their hearts beating, hoping that they will find the gifts they have requested, placed at the foot of the tree the next morning.

The family is at the heart of Mauritian culture and Mauritian families are happy to gather around a meal for Christmas dinner or for the traditional lunch or dinner at the grandparents' house where we will entertain with great ceremony. At the table you can find dishes such as: roasted turkey or roasted chicken accompanied by salads or gratins, or seafood with all kinds of sauces and as desert the essential Christmas log and to be more original; ice cream accompanied by a seasonal fruit salad. The Mauritian Christmas celebration would be incomplete without its family anecdotes, stories of years gone by, laughter guaranteed and end on a high note: the breathtaking fireworks and firecrackers!

Christmas Board Game

Here is a Question - Answer game. It is a ludo type game.
dice used to play.

Start	① What day is Christmas on?	② Who lives on the North Pole?	③ What are the colours of Christmas?	④ What do we hang on the fireplace?
⑨ What do you call a manmade snow?	⑧ What do we put on Christmas tree?	⑦ What do Santas helpers make?	⑥ Roll again	⑤ How does Santa travel?
⑩ What are the animals that help Santa?	⑪ Who are Santa's helpers?	⑫ What is a candy cane?	⑬ What is call the Christmas song?	⑭ What do you buy a present for?
⑲ What is a Gingerbread house?	⑱ What month in Christmas in?	⑰ What do we put under the tree?	⑯ Jump ahead 4 spaces.	⑮ What do we leave for Santa to eat?
⑳ Name to Christmas plants?	㉑ What do we eat on Christmas?	㉒ What do we hang on our door?	㉓ What would you like for Christmas?	㉔ Go forward 4 spaces
FINISH	㉘ What song do we sing at Christmas?	㉖ Name 2 Christmas movie?	㉗ What Cookies do you eat in your country?	㉕ What cookie looks like a man?

Christmas in Togo

This Compassion centre in southern Togo knows how to throw a memorable celebration at Christmastime.

Most years, the community prepares with excitement for the joyful celebration of Jesus' birth. Children receive new clothes and shoes while the centre is filled with the sounds of music, cheerful voices and party whistles, and the smell of freshly cooked food. As toys are unwrapped and shared, the excitement peaks with children shouting over the music, laughing and dancing with joy.

Children and their families receive special food kits, home visits and gifts delivered to their doors.

Several Yule traditions are familiar to the modern celebration of Christmas, such as Yule Log, the custom of burning a large wooden log on the fire at Christmas; or indeed carol singing, which is surprisingly a very ancient tradition.

This picture has a boy and __________.

There is a __________ behind the boy.

Santa has given ______ gifts to the boy.

It's ________ behind.

Boy is ________ the gift car given by Santa.

Homemade Peanut Clusters

Ingredients:

1 Package of white almond bark (usually 12 squares)

1 bag of semisweet chocolate chips

1 lb Virginia peanuts

Directions:

1. Melt almond bark in microwave for 1 minute on High

2. Stir. Then add chocolate chips, melt for 1min 30 seconds on High

3. Stir. Melt for another minute or until all melted.

4. Add peanuts and mix well.

5. Drop spoonful onto waxed paper. Let cool and harden.

Christmas in Djibouti

Christmas in Djibouti is celebrated by a handful of Christians residing in the country. The major religion in Djibouti is Islam. There is relatively a very small Christian community living at Djibouti.

Christmas at Djibouti is celebrated with enough zeal and enthusiasm by those observing the religion of Christianity, as all the churches get decorated with candles and lights. Midnight prayers are held and small children singing choirs are joined by the grown-ups on this auspicious day. The choirs and songs that are sung on Christmas in Djibouti is usually performed in different languages like Arabic, Somali and Afar.

Match some of the workers here and their passion for work?

pilot

scientist

computer programmer

teacher

doctor

police

librarian

gardener

cook

fire fighter

1. I want to be a _____________________ because I like catch the criminals.

2. I want to be a _____________________ because I am good at science.

3. I want to be a _____________________ because I love children.

4. I want to be a _____________________ because I enjoy protecting people.

5. I want to be a _____________________ because I love books and reading.

6. I want to be a _____________________ because I enjoy creating video games.

7. I want to be a _____________________ because I enjoy working with food.

8. I want to be a _____________________ because I like to heal patients.

9. I want to be a _____________________ because I enjoy working outside.

10. I want to be a _____________________ because I love to fly high.

Christmas in Angola

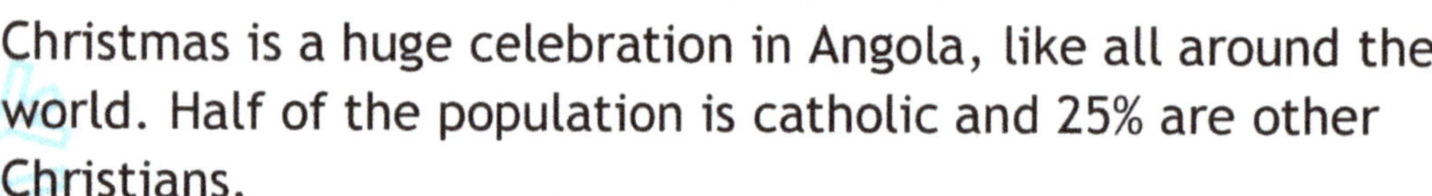

Christmas is a huge celebration in Angola, like all around the world. Half of the population is catholic and 25% are other Christians.

Natives decorate their houses to welcome travellers back to home to make occasion memorable. The main decoration is Nativity Scene (Presépio), trees are also decorated with stockings and other stuff. Travelers use the holiday to enjoy big celebrations and meet their family and friends. For the mighty celebration, public holidays are announced for schools, offices, and other workers.

Mass of Christmas include midnight mass service on Christmas eve, which is often broadcasted on national television for people who cannot join church in person. Special church services are also offered for people to join religious rituals.

Shopping centres and companies offers promos and reduce prices on the objects for people to enjoy their shopping.

Gifts are a big part of Christmas celebration as everyone buys gifts for their friends and family in the spirit of Christmas.

In Angola Portuguese 'Feliz Nata' is used instead of Marry/happy Christmas.

Special meals like 'pirão' or 'funge', which is served with rice, spaghetti, french fries, turkey, fried chicken, 'ozido de bacalhau', 'calulu', 'mufete', and Bolo Rei cake are famous to serve family and friends on Christmas.

 **Here is a design outline of some of the Christmas elements, you fill it with right colour scheme**

Letter to Santa

Dear Santa,

My name is _______________________ and I am

__________ years old.

This year, I have been _______________ with family and friends.

For Christmas, please bring me

____

____

____

____

____

____

With love from _______________________________

Christmas in Swaziland

In Swaziland Christmas is on the 25th of December. It is a beautiful time of year, where Christians get together with friends and families to celebrate Christmas.

The day starts with a midnight mass in church, then is followed by a meal at home.

Children take this opportunity to open presents, and sing Christmas carols.

Here is a colourless picture of the birth of Jesus.
Will you colour here?

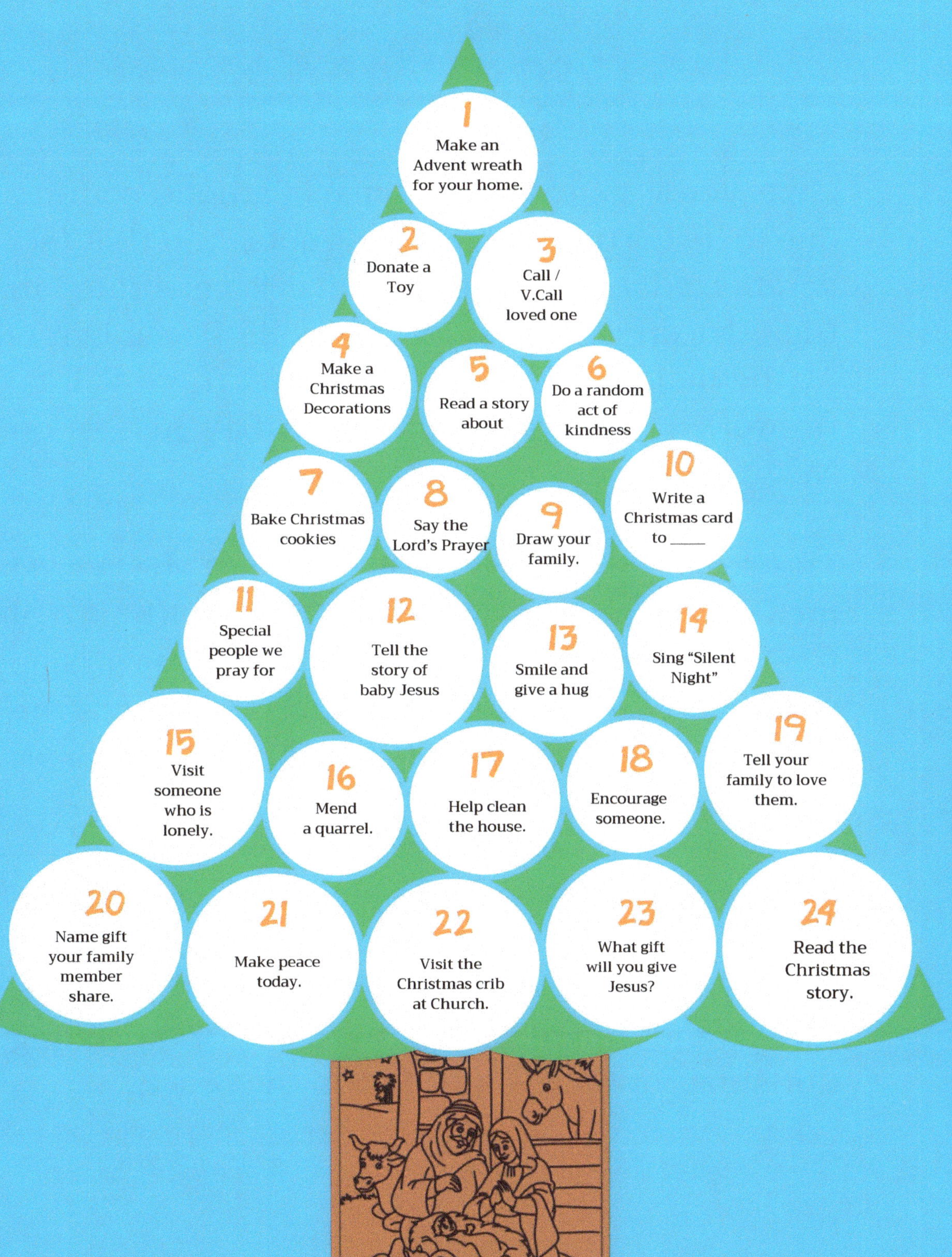

Family Advent Poster

1
Make an Advent wreath for your home.

2
Donate a Toy

3
Call / V.Call loved one

4
Make a Christmas Decorations

5
Read a story about

6
Do a random act of kindness

7
Bake Christmas cookies

8
Say the Lord's Prayer

9
Draw your family.

10
Write a Christmas card to ____

11
Special people we pray for

12
Tell the story of baby Jesus

13
Smile and give a hug

14
Sing "Silent Night"

15
Visit someone who is lonely.

16
Mend a quarrel.

17
Help clean the house.

18
Encourage someone.

19
Tell your family to love them.

20
Name gift your family member share.

21
Make peace today.

22
Visit the Christmas crib at Church.

23
What gift will you give Jesus?

24
Read the Christmas story.

Christmas in Cape Verde

Cape Verde is a strong Roman Catholic country due to its Portuguese colonial roots. And that fact is reflected in the way Christmas is celebrated in this African island nation every 25 December. ... At the major hotels in Cape Verde, there will be fireworks displays on Christmas Day just as on New Year's Eve.

The local Christmas traditions in Cape Verde include extended meals in the family with typical food and drinks from Cape Verde such as grogue or ponche. Like in Western countries, there's the culture of making presents for your beloved ones and your family.

In December, the islands enjoy average highs of 27°C. With very little rain, the sunshine is guaranteed, making December ideal for beach lovers and families. It's perfect for spending Christmas or New Year's Day on the beach.

Based on the information on the previous page, fill in the blanks below.

- Cape Verde is a strong _______________ Catholic country due to its _________________ colonial roots.

- At the major hotels in Cape Verde, there will be ________________ displays.

- In Cape Verde include extended meals in the family with typical food and drinks from Cape Verde such as _______________ or _______________.

- In December, the islands enjoy average highs of _____________. With very little rain.

- It's perfect for spending Christmas or New Year's Day on the beach.

Christmas food Anagram

a b c e e i n r r r s ______________________

i m n s t ______________________

a c c e h l o o t ______________________

a g r v y ______________________

a l n s t u w ______________________

a m s y ______________________

c e i k o o s ______________________

d d g i n p u ______________________

e k r t u y ______________________

f f g i n s t u ______________________

cookies

walnuts

yams

cranberries

gravy

pudding

stuffing

chocolate

turkey

mints

Christmas in Morocco

A number of Christian churches scattered throughout the country celebrate mass on Christmas Day, and welcome foreigners to join the celebration. It's estimated that around 100,000 people in Morocco celebrate the holiday, and many of them are of French descent.

Even in December, the weather is pretty friendly in Morocco. There's a bit more rain in the winter than there is in the summer, but the temperatures are quite mild overall.

The Moroccan city boasts blissful weather and some of the world's most magical holiday decorations. ...

The French have long known about the holiday wonders of the Red City, named for its ochre-coloured town walls, flocking here to make merry and bright from Christmas Eve through New Year's Day.

Santa Cookies

Ingredients:

- Nutter Butter cookies
- White chocolate chips
- Mini chocolate chips
- Red cinnamon candy or mini red M&M's
- Mini marshmallows cut in halves or quarters
- Red sugar

Directions:

1. Melt white chocolate chips.

2. Dip Nutter Butter into chocolate a little more than halfway to make the beard. Let dry (it does not take long).

3. Dip top in about two lines (grid on N.B.) and then roll into red sugar across the top, but not all the way.

4. Immediately attach marshmallow to the melted choc on the hat.

5. Using melted white chocolate as glue, dip mini choc chip in and then attach to cookie as eyes.

6. Repeat for nose with cinnamon candy dot or M&M. (I often just place the nose on when I make the beard, at the top to save time.)

Here is Santa's face outline. You can
colour this face or decorate it.

Christmas in Equatorial Guinea

Equatorial Guinea is mostly Roman Catholic, so the country celebrates Christmas every December 25. Apart from Christian festivities, traditional celebrations are also held like the dance known as balélé in the Bioko region. In the cities, friends and families celebrate together by eating, drinking and exchanging gifts.

For the Churches, this is a time for reflection, and most of the churches and organisations have prepared special activities, with choruses, moments of reflection, and retreat, Mass and veneration.

Like other countries, they shop early. Since most of the country is Roman Catholic, they celebrate on December 25 along with Christian festivities and traditional celebrations. They also have a dance called the balele in the Bioko region.

The government used to donate gifts and food which is taken to the elderly and the most disadvantaged population.

On the day itself it is mostly spent visiting friends and family. They exchange gifts and share meals.

For their houses they put up some lights, ribbons, and balloons.

The Carol Singers

There are four penguins named Micky, Fred, Rob and Eve who are fond of singing Christmas carols before the inhabitants of the ice pack, where they live. Every time they sang, they received a golden star, which they put up on their Christmas tree.

One Christmas eve, Micky catches a terrible cold and starts sneezing. He tells his fellow singers that they will have to sing without him that year as he is unwell. "No, that's not possible," said the other three. But they realise that the inhabitants of the ice pack looked forward to their performance every year and would be terribly disappointed if they didn't sing.

The penguins decide to approach Doctor Lolo and ask to heal Micky soon. The doctor thinks for a while and tells them that the only way to get Micky better was by using the golden seaweed, which could be found in the Indian Ocean.

The penguins realised that the Indian Ocean is far away from them and that it would not be possible for them to get the seaweed in such a short time. Fred is tearful, and his tears fell in the water below, which Pincho, an ice fish, feels on his body. He swims up to the penguins and asks them the reason for their sadness.

On hearing their problem, Pincho says, "Wait! If it is the Indian Ocean, I have an idea." He has friends and family spread across all the great seas of the world and begins to send messages to them.

The message is passed on from one fish to another, across the Arctic Ocean and the Pacific Ocean, before finally reaching the butterflyfish in the Indian Ocean. The butterflyfish looks for the golden seaweed, high and low. When he finally finds it, he passes it across till it reaches Pincho.

The penguins are overjoyed, and they ask the doctor to prepare the medicine from it. Micky drinks the medicine in one gulp and his original voice returns in a jiffy. The Christmas carol show is a hit, and the penguins tell everyone how Pincho helped them in finding the golden seaweed.

Through this story, your kids can learn about teamwork and how by helping each other, we can bring true happiness to the world.

Q: What were the names of the penguins that sang Christmas Carol?

A:____

____

____

Q: What did they get when they sang carol?

A:____

____

____

Q: What did Mickey need to heal, and where could he be found?

A:____

____

____

Q: Fred's tears fell on whom?

A:____

____

____

Q: What did you learn from this story?

A:____

____

____

Who discovered seaweed and where?

A:____

____

____

Christmas in Eritrea

Christmas is a popular holiday in Eritrea but it's not celebrated on the 25th of December. It is celebrated on January 7th. This is because the vast majority of Eritrean Christians are Orthodox and they follow the Geez calendar.

This traditional is similar to the Ethopian Christmas, page 13.

Many people take part in a special Advent fast during the 43 days before Christmas. It starts on 25th November and is known as the 'Fast of the Prophets' (Tsome Nebiyat).

During this time, traditionally only one vegan meal is eaten each day. It's a vegan meal because during the fast, foods including meat, dairy, eggs and wine aren't eaten.

Unlike the U.S. and other parts of the world in Eritrea, Christmas comes second to Easter.

Some may even decorate Christmas Trees and exchange gifts. This tradition is fairly new, but things are changing and the Western world's influence is hard to resist.

Abstract Colourful Homemade Christmas Card

We love making our own Christmas cards, but we want them to be easy to make – as making a number of them can become quite a chore if they aren't easy. This card includes a bit of colouring, but it will be a relaxing experience.

What you need:
·Paper for the card or blank cards
·White card stick
·Colouring supplies
·Black marker
·Ruler (or just use paper to make straight lines)
·Round cap for the circle
·Glue
·Scissors

Direction:

Take a sheet of A4 / letter sized construction paper in your favourite colour and fold it in half. Cut along the fold. Place the folded card on top of white cardstock and use it as a stencil to cut a white rectangle. Place the folded card on top of white cardstock and use it as a stencil to cut a white rectangle. Draw a rectangle inside the white rectangle with a black marker. Take one of the two halves and fold it in half again. This will make one card base (make another one from the other half if you like). Draw a rectangle inside the white rectangle with a black marker. If you have a bolder black marker, use it to draw a tree shape – keep it simple, draw a triangle and a small rectangle under it. Now draw lines across the rectangle – randomly. You can also add some circles. We used the glue cap as our circle stencil. Apply glue on the back of the white rectangle and glue it on your card. Next comes the colouring. We coloured the shapes inside the tree with different shades of green and blue-green. We coloured the outside with different shades of purple. Last but not least, add a special note inside the card. All done, your geometric Abstract Colourful Homemade Christmas Card is all done. Now just place it inside an envelope and give it to an awesome person.

Christmas in Gabon

The Episcopal Conference of Gabon estimates approximately 80 percent of the population is Christian.

Of the Christian population, approximately two-thirds are Roman Catholic and one-third Protestant, which includes evangelical and awakening churches.

Christmas Day is December 25. Many Christmas traditions include eating special foods and drinks. Sharing family dinners and special treats last the entire Christmas season.

Different areas of Gabon celebrate slightly differently and also incorporate traditions of indigenous religions into the celebrations.

Christmas Crossword Puzzle

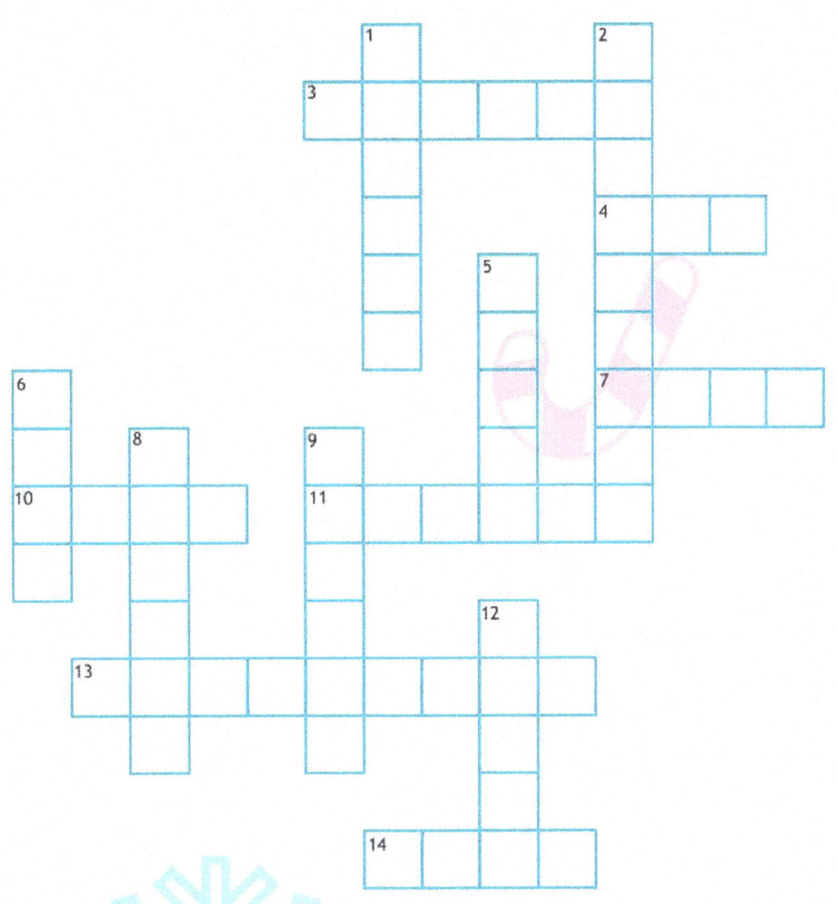

DOWN

1. Animal that Mary rode to Bethlehem

2. The night before Christmas

5. The book where the Christmas story is found

6. These three ______________ men brought gifts

8. An animal's feeding trough

9. Mary, Joseph and Jesus were a ______________

12. Christmas is the celebration of the birth of ______________

ACROSS

3. Mary's husband

4. There was no room at the ______________

7. The mother of Jesus

10. Led the wise men to Jesus

11. Announced Jesus' birth to the shepherds

13. The town where Jesus was born

14. The direction that the three wise men came from

Answers

Down: 1. Donkey 2. Christmas Eve. 5. Bible 6. Wise 8. Manger 9. Family 12. Jesus

Across: 3. Joseph 4. Inn 7. Mary 10. Star 11 Angels 13. Bethlehem 14. East

 Here is a design outline of some of the Christmas elements, you fill it with right colour scheme

Christmas in Lesotho

Christmas in Lesotho is celebrated with a public holiday every 25 December, as it is in a majority of countries around the world.

This Christian festivity commemorates the birth of Jesus and is part of a 22-28-day season in the Christian calendar known as Advent. Lesotho is a predominantly Christian country.

The Christmas Holiday celebration begins as a homecoming throughout December. On Christmas Eve, we will go to church; usually the entire family attends, with the exception of some of the younger men.

From about 10pm until 4 or 5am we will sing and pray, read the bible and celebrate the birth of Christ.

Christmas Fudge

Ingredients:

- 1 cup sugar
- 1/2 cup butter
- 1/2 cup heavy cream
- 1/8 tsp salt
- 2 cups powdered sugar
- 1 tsp vanilla
- 1/2 cup red candied cherries, chopped
- 1/2 cup green candied cherries, chopped

Directions:

1. Spray an 8x8" baking dish with cooking spray.

2. In a large saucepan, bring the sugar, butter, cream and salt to a boil over medium heat, stirring frequently. Let boil for 5 minutes, stirring constantly. Remove from heat and slowly add the powdered sugar and vanilla, stirring until smooth and well combined. Stir in the cherries until evenly distributed.

3. Spoon into baking dish and chill for 1 hour or until firm. Cut into squares. Store in an airtight container.

Christmas in Liberia

Christmas on December 25 is the nation's favourite holiday, with preparations for the big day lasting weeks in advance. It's a secular and religious event, with Liberia's Muslims celebrating with special meals and family get-togethers, and Christians attending church services.

English is the official language of Liberia. In what country do they say "nollaig nait cugat" for Merry Christmas? Irish Gaelic would normally be "Nollaig shona dhuit!" (Merry Christmas to you).

Therefore, our major purpose for Christmas is to go to church, to worship Him and to praise Him for His salvation that He offered us. Together, we also prepare a good meal for the Christmas and we share with others.

The majority of Liberians claim to be Christians (about 80%). Church attendance is a priority and after the mass or Sunday service, people spill out onto the roads in their Sunday finery, greeting friends, blessing each other, and searching for a ride home. Christmas Day is spent with the family and people go all out to enjoy a nice meal and share some small gifts for the children.

Family time is very important and after sharing the special meal, families will go to the beach or somewhere special to visit and pass the time together. Liberians celebrate Christmas on the public holiday.

Here is a picture of a penguin with a graph. Draw a picture on a given graph as it is?

Christmas in Malawi

Malawi's Christmas traditions are much like our Christian traditions around the world. Also, they celebrate Christmas on December 25 in their calendar, which is probably January 7 for us.

There is a lot of singing, dancing and dramas which are fantastic to watch. Malawians give simple, often handmade gifts and give verbal greetings.

Most people in Malawi speak Chichewa or Tumbuka.

In Malawi, Christmas is celebrated through December 31st, when communities come together for the new year celebration but don't forget Boxing Day!

There is no celebration in Malawi quite like Chilimike. The Chilimike celebrations are Malawi's New Year festivities, enjoyed on January 1st as a public holiday.

Gifts are presented to each other, and families visit each other.

Most gifts are handmade like the Christmas angel ornament made in Malawi.

On Christmas day, they eat roasted meat, banana bread, sweet potato cookies, peanut puffs and banana fritters.

STAY HOME! STAY SAFE!
In this Christmas I did 5 things to keep myself and other safe.

Complete the drawing of
the fox below and colour

Christmas in Rwanda

On Christmas Eve, the streets of Kigali and other cities traditionally fill up with those singing Christmas songs on their way to and from church.

Church, family, and food are easily the three key pillars of Christmas in Rwanda.

Rwanda has very little commercialisation of Christmas compared to other countries.

You won't find many Santa's, reindeer, and Christmas trees. And many families don't even exchange gifts.

Instead, 25 December is focused on family and a festive meal together.

Rwandans who are accustomed to Christmas exchange gifts. However, a typical Rwandan tradition for Christmas is a day full of relaxation, prayer, and goat brochettes (kebabs).

There is also a traditional food of Isombe, which is mashed cassava leaves and green bananas cooked in tomato sauce.

Here are some pictures drawn in the shape of a square, circle, triangle and rectangle. You count the number of shapes in front of each picture.

Some of the numbers are given to add up and the
solutions are given below. Will you solve it?

4+8
8+7
15+5
6+10
9+2
5+2
15
20
16
7
12
11

Christmas in Senegal

When Muslims celebrate their holidays, the Christians participate, and vice versa. It shows the social cohesion and the strength of Senegal. While Muslim Senegal's Christmas is limited to the commercial and secular, it is still a celebration of the Christian holiday and the unity of this West African nation.

Senegal, a moderate country along Africa's western coast, has long been a place where Christians and Muslims have coexisted peacefully. Most Christians here are Catholic and live in the south of country and in the capital.

Signs of Christmas are prevalent in this tropical seaside capital.

Green and flocked plastic trees of every size are sold on street corners alongside Nescafe carts and vendors splitting open coconuts.

Santa Claus, in this former French colony also makes the rounds at upscale shopping centres and grocery stores in the weeks before Christmas.

students all get together for a Christmas party the weekend before the holiday with their parents. The teachers put presents under a tree and Santa Claus shows up to hand them out.

HOW TO MAKE

A REINDEER HAT

This quick and easy reindeer craft is one of
favourites all kids. It only takes a few minutes to
complete, and kids of all ages absolutely adore it.

Materials:

- Construction Paper
- Googly Eyes
- Pom Poms
- Scissors
- Tape or Glue
- Marker

Direction:

Step 1: Cut a sheet of brown construction paper into
several 2 inch strips.

Step 2: Tape (or glue) two of the construction paper
strips together to form the base of the reindeer hat. Use
your child's head as a guide for the size.

Step 3: On another sheet of brown construction paper,
trace your child's hands.

Step 4: Cut out the hands, and attach them to the base
of the reindeer hat. These will become the antlers.

Step 5: Add googly eyes and a red pom-pom nose to
complete the face of the reindeer. Hand over the
adorable hat to your little one, and enjoy the cuteness.

Below is the addition-subtraction puzzle. Will you solve it?
5
+3
-2
+4
-6
+8
-1
+9
-7
-1
+4
124

Christmas in Seychelles

Christmas is a very special time in Seychelles and like a lot of other countries, radio stations play carols throughout the Christmas period. Many people paint their houses and hang new curtains and decorations for Christmas. Most families spend Christmas Day at home with friends and family members.

Thinking about a holiday during the Christmas Season to the Seychelles? Then what are you waiting for to book it? The Seychelles islands propose a great escape from the hassle of bustle of the festive season. Rather than being cold near your fire, enjoy a wonderful hot Christmas day at the beach getting a suntan.

Like everywhere Christmas is celebrated around globe 0n 25th of December, Seychelles also celebrate Christmas like every other country. People attend service, feast, present gifts and also evening celebrations.

Every year lot of tourists visit Seychelles to enjoy Christmas here. the whole town is decorated with colourful lights and the trees are decorated with lights. it's truly an awesome view, starting from first week of December till new year, whole town decorated.

The houses in the mountains with colourful lights steal your minds. you can find a lot of colour lighted Christmas statues in town to take photos. Moreover, most of the restaurants in Seychelles provide special Christmas buffet and meal throughout the month.

Up to 100 dots are given here. You can joint them and
complete the drawing of the giraffe and colour it.

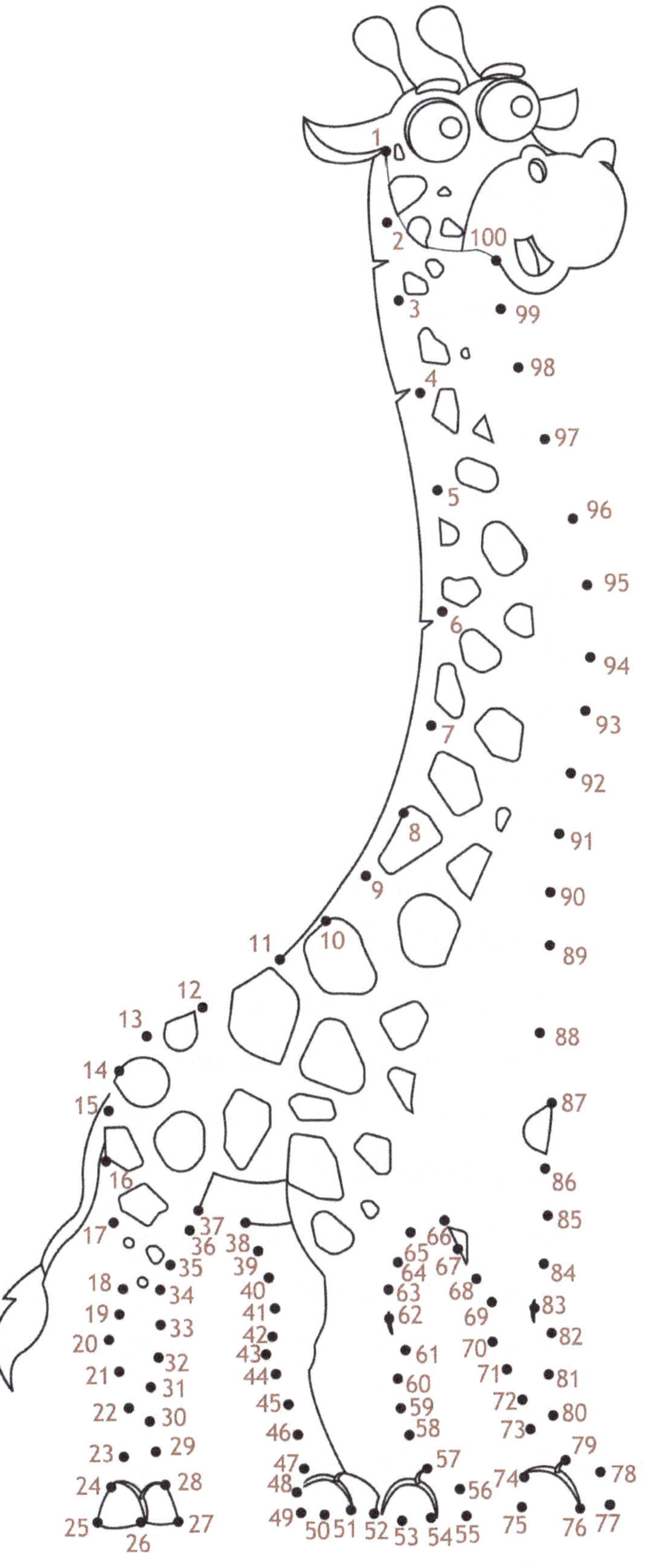

Christmas in Sierra Leone

Sierra Leone street carnivals celebrate warm Christmas with food and music. Sierra Leone's capital, Freetown, has an old tradition of Christmas Street carnivals organised in various neighbourhoods across the city. Residents gather on the streets enjoying food and music for a month-long celebration.

Christmas is celebrated by 29°C in Freetown. The city is bustling with Christmas activities and, in some neighbourhoods, the streets are crowded, if not blocked, for the yearly street carnivals, an event which takes place in various spots around the capital throughout December.

"People just enjoy the food and music outside. Every street wants to have a carnival. People will set up a stage, put chairs outside. They come well dressed to dance, eat Sierra Leonean food, like pepper soup, cassava leaves," says artist Tutie Haffner, who has organised a few street carnivals in the past.

The street carnivals in Freetown have been running for the past 30 years, with increased popularity in the last 15 years. Most of them are free, with some contribution requested to cover costs.

The carnival crowd quite enjoy music from Sierra Leone and Nigeria. And they are quite partial to gumbe music as well as traditional genres belonging to various ethnic groups – for example, the mende music of the Mende people, the bubu of the Temne people or the milo jazz emanating from the Krio culture.

A younger generation of Sierra Leonean musicians enjoy experimenting with bembeske, a fusion of the traditional genres.

A	B	C	D	E	F	G	H	I	J	K	L	M

N	O	P	Q	R	S	T	U	V	W	X	Y	Z

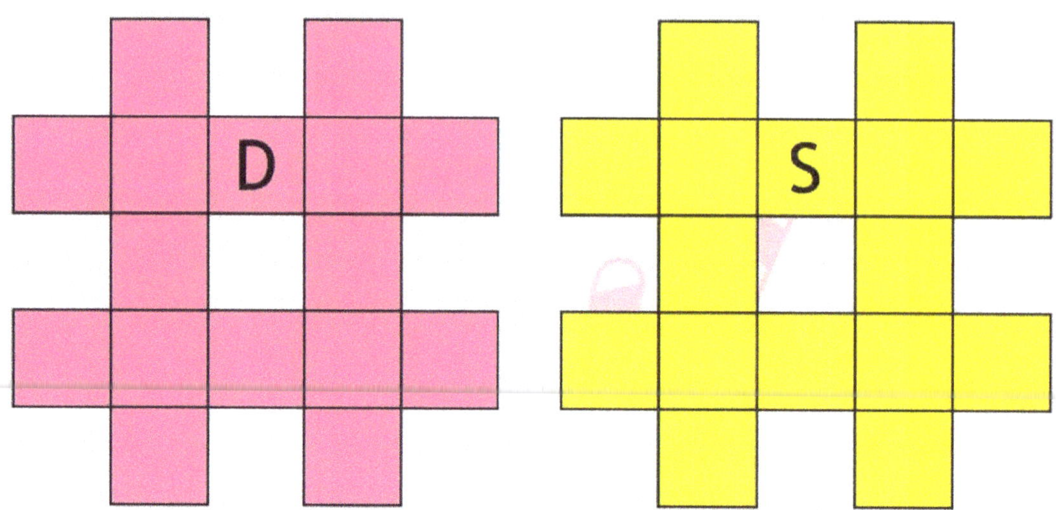

3 letter words

TEA

FOG

HEN

DOT

5 letter words

ATTIC

BEACH

BEGIN

FENCE

FIFTY

OTHER

OTTER

RIDER

Crossword1
Across: RIDER, FOG, ATTIC. Down: FIFTY, DOT, BEGIN
Crossword2
Across: OTHER, TEA, FENCE. Down: OTTER, HEN, BEACH

Word search puzzle.

Use 'Christmas in South Africa' information to search the words.

B	M	O	P	N	Q	T	P	S	G
A	D	U	P	U	D	D	I	N	G
R	A	S	L	I	T	O	R	L	T
B	O	G	R	I	L	L	K	L	U
E	C	A	P	E	T	O	W	N	R
C	B	T	V	A	U	X	A	P	K
U	R	V	D	U	C	K	K	L	E
E	A	O	C	A	P	E	T	U	Y
O	A	Y	B	N	Q	L	W	M	B
H	I	Z	C	A	M	P	I	N	G

DUCK, GRILL, PLUM, BRAAI, PUDDING, CAMPING, TURKEY, HOLIDAY, BARBECUE, CAPETOWN

Which African countries do not celebrate Christmas?

Christmas is celebrated differently all over the world, with most countries ringing in the holiday season with their own traditions and practices. But of the nearly 200 countries on Earth, a handful of non-Christian nations don't recognise Christmas and have no form of public holiday or observation to mark the nativity of Jesus Christ.

Algeria

Another Muslim-majority nation, Algeria has not observed Christmas in any official capacity since it gained its independence from France, a mostly Catholic nation, in 1962.

Comoros

At 98% Sunni Muslim, the Comoros archipelago in the Indian Ocean takes a firm stance against Christianity. World Atlas reports that the open practice of Christianity is prohibited, and Comoros has "been on the World Watch list for the past 22 years for the persecution of Christians".

Libya

What's left of the government in this lawless, predominantly Muslim nation does not observe Christmas. However, 24 December is the country's Independence Day, so expect a party then instead.

Mauritania

The government of Mauritania, despite having a small population of Christians within its borders, chooses not to recognise them at all, with the most recent census claiming that 100% of the country is Muslim.

Somalia

In 2015, Somalia, which adopted Sharia law in 2009, banned the celebration of Christmas outright, warning that such Christian festivities could threaten the nation's Muslim faith.

Tunisia

Although Christmas is not banned here, Tunisia has almost no public celebrations of the holiday and it is a regular workday for the country.

GINGERBREAD

With Best

Wishes To You

A Merry

Christmas